Understanding Christianity
キリスト教を理解する

An 8-week Course on Foundational Principles
基本原則を学ぶ 8 週間のコース

Christie P. Moon
クリスティ・P・ムーン

CCD Press

UNDERSTANDING CHRISTIANITY
An 8-week Course on Foundational Principles

Additional copies of this resource may be obtained at www.crossculturaldiscipleship.com.

ISBN-13: 978-0-578-70519-4

Published by CCD Press
Yokota AB, Japan
www.crossculturaldiscipleship.com

Translated by Akiyo Stier (スティアー明代)
Illustrated by Minami Nanami (みなみななみ)

Printed in the United States of America

Acknowledgments
謝辞

Thank you to everyone who contributed to the development of this book. Many of our friends, family members and spiritual leaders generously gave their time to help review, translate, and illustrate the content. Their expertise and skills were essential in this process. Many others have prayed for the writing team and the future readers.

I would like to extend a special thanks to Akiyo Stier for translating this book, to Minami Nanami for illustrating, to Patrick Snow for providing support and guidance as the publishing coach and to my husband, Travis Moon, for all of his support throughout the process. I would also like to thank Aoi Takano, Deborah Sylvester, Ethan Moon, Gloria Bun, Kevin Galvin, Minami Nanami, Tom and Chika Cotton, Travis Moon and Yuri Ayliffe for helping to edit and review the book.

Words alone cannot truly capture the magnitude of your contributions. We prayed for help throughout each step of this process, and you were each an answer to those prayers. The Lord handpicked this team, and it is evident in the quality of the final product. It has been such a blessing to work with you and to see your hearts for the readers and passion for sharing the gospel with the Japanese people.

この本の作成に貢献したすべての人に感謝します。私たちの多くの友人、家族、精神的な指導者が、内容のレビュー、翻訳、説明を磨くために時間を惜しみなく使ってくれました。これら一人ひとりの専門知識やスキルは、作成のプロセスに不可欠でした。また多くの人々が、執筆チームと未来の読者のために祈ってくれました。

この本を翻訳してくれたスティアー明代さん、挿絵を描いてくれたみなみななみさん、出版のコーチとしてサポートとガイドをしてくれたパトリック・スノーさん、そしてプロセス全体にわたってサポートしてくれた私の夫であるトラビス・ムーンさんに心から感謝します。 また、この本の編集とレビューをしてくれたタカノアオイさん、デボラ・シルベスターさん、イーサン・ムーンさん、グロリア・ブーンさん、ケビン・ガルビンさん、みなみななみさん、トム・コットンさん、コットン千佳さん、トラビス・ムーン、アイリフ百吏さんにも感謝します。

言葉だけではみなさんの貢献の大きさを正確に伝えることはできません。私たちは、このプロセスにおける各ステップで助けが与えられることを祈りました。そしてみなさん一人一人が祈りに対する答えでした。主はこのチームを注意深く選ばれました。そのことは仕上がったこの本の質を見れば明白です。皆さんと一緒に働くことができたこと、また、読者への気持ちと、福音を日本の皆さんと共有したいという情熱を感じることができたことは、素晴らしい恵でした。

CONTENTS
目次

Introduction
はじめに

There is one God, and He cares about you very much and wants to have a relationship with you. This book is an invitation to get to know Him. It is not a coincidence that you are here today reading this. God loves you and He is pursuing you. He has special plans for you. You exist for a reason and you have a purpose.

Let the words of the Bible and the story of Jesus speak into your life. Ask questions, think deeply about what Scripture says and start building a relationship with the Lord. Take advantage of this opportunity to learn about Him. Your Bible study teacher and your church are here to help you.

Christie P. Moon

神は唯一のお方で、あなたをとても気遣い、あなたと交わりを持ちたいと願っておられます。この本は、神を知ることへの招待状です。今日あなたがこれを読んでいるのは偶然ではありません。神はあなたを愛し、あなたを追い求めておられます。神はあなたに特別な計画を持っておられます。あなたが存在しているのには理由があり、また目的があるのです。

聖書の言葉とイエスの生涯があなたの人生に語りかけてくれますように。質問をしたりして、聖書が述べていることについて深く考え、主との関係を築き始めてください。この機会を利用して、神について学びましょう。バイブルスタディのリーダーとあなたの教会は、あなたを助けるためにいます。

クリスティ・P・ムーン

THE GOSPEL MESSAGE
福音のメッセージ

We will start by looking into the foundational message of Christianity. Your weekly homework and group discussions will go deeper into this message. The gospel refers to the "good news," which is the story of Jesus.

まず、最初にキリスト教の基本的なメッセージを学びましょう。毎週の宿題やグループディスカッションでは、このメッセージの内容についてより深く学んでいきます。福音とはイエスの生涯である「良き知らせ」を指しています。

THE GOSPEL MESSAGE
福音のメッセージ

There is one God. He is the only God. He is pure, good, and loving. He is holy and set apart from all evil. God is sovereign and all-powerful. He loves you and wants to have a relationship with you. He is present everywhere. He created the world and He created you.

In the beginning, when God created mankind, there was harmony between God and man. Then the first people fell into temptation and disobeyed God. This rebellion was the first sin against God, which led to separation from Him. People still disobey God today. One act of disobedience separates us from God, because God is pure and holy. We cannot reconcile with God by our own works.

The good news is that God loved mankind too much to let the relationship stay broken. He sent His Son Jesus down to the earth to save us. Jesus lived a perfect life and did not sin, so He was able to pay the price for our sin. The punishment for sin is death. Jesus took this punishment on the cross for us, giving His life as a sacrifice to redeem ours.

Three days after He died, He defeated death and rose again by the power of God. His resurrection was a miracle. He appeared to many people after He rose from the dead, and then He ascended into heaven. Our God is one God, who is the Father in heaven, the Son Jesus who came down to earth, and the Holy Spirit. God offers reconciliation in our relationship with Him, and eternal life, to all who believe in Jesus.

唯一の神が存在します。彼は清く、善良で、愛情深い方です。彼は聖い方であり、すべての悪から離れた存在です。神は全てにおいて主権を持った強い方です。あなたを愛し、あなたと個人的な交わりを持ちたいと思っておられます。また彼はあらゆる場所において存在しておられます。神は全世界を創造し、あなたを創造しました。

初めに神が人類を創造したとき、神と人の間には調和がありました。しかし最初の人々は誘惑に陥り、神に背きました。この反抗は神に対する最初の罪であり、神からの分離をもたらしました。今日でも人々は神に背きます。神は清く神聖であるがゆえに背信の行為は神からの分離をもたらします。私たちは行いにより神と和解することはできません。

幸いなことに、神は人類を深く愛しておられるので壊れた関係をそのままにはされませんでした。彼は私たちを救うため、自分の御子イエスをこの世に遣わされました。イエスは完全な人生を生き、全く罪を犯さなかったので、私たちの罪の代価を支払うことができました。罪に対する罰は死です。イエスは私たちを救うため、私たちの代わりに十字架にかかり、自らの命を犠牲として捧げてくださいました。

死から三日後、彼は死を打ち負かし、神の力によってよみがえりました。彼の復活は奇跡でした。イエスは死からよみがえった後、多くの人々の前に現れ、そして天に昇られました。唯一の存在である私たちの神は、天におられる父、地上に降りてきた御子イエス、そして聖霊です。神は、イエスを信じるすべての人に、関係を回復されるべく和解を差し伸べ、そして永遠のいのちを与えてくださいます。

THE GOSPEL MESSAGE
福音のメッセージ

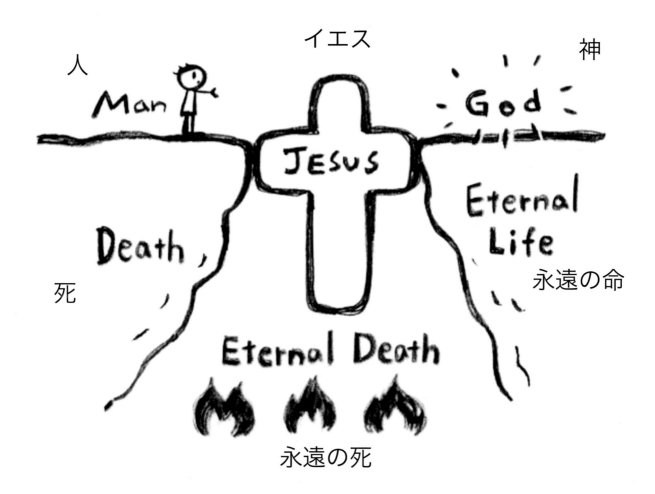

This illustration shows the separation from God that exists because of sin. Death is the consequence of sin. No amount of good works can help someone to escape this end result. Salvation through Jesus is the only way to be reconciled to God. Those who believe in Jesus will gain eternal life.

　この図は、罪が原因で起こった神からの分離を示しています。死は罪の結果です。自分は良い行いをしたからといってこの結末から逃れることはできません。イエスを通しての救いこそが、神と和解するための唯一の方法です。イエスを信じる者は永遠の命を得るのです。

USING THIS BOOK
この本の使い方

This workbook is intended for use in Bible study groups with one or more students, led by a Christian teacher. Get started with the following steps:

1. **Get a copy of the Bible in your own language.** You can find a paper copy at a church or Christian bookstore. Digital copies are also available.

2. **Read the guides in the back of the book.** Read through the "About the Bible" section. Ensure you know how to look up Bible verses. Review the "Christian Vocabulary List" to learn new terms. Teachers, read the "Teacher's Guide."

3. **Start the workbook.** Complete the "Study," "Reflect," and "Review" sections individually.

4. **Meet as a group.** At your weekly meeting, review the homework to ensure that everyone understands it. Go through the discussion questions together.

5. **Complete the "Live It Out" section.** Review the weekly challenge as a group. Some may be appropriate to do together. Others may be better to do individually during the week.

このワークブックは、クリスチャンのリーダーと生徒の一人対一人か、複数人のグループでの学びを想定して作成されています。下記の手順で始めてください。

1. **自分の言語で書かれた聖書を入手してください。** 教会やキリスト教書店で聖書を見つけることができます。 デジタル版も利用可能です。

2. **本の裏にあるガイドを読んでください。** 「聖書について」を読んでください。 聖書の聖句を調べる方法を確認してください。 「クリスチャン語彙録」を確認して、新しい用語を学習します。 リーダーは、「リーダーのためのガイド」を読んでください。

3. **ワークブックを開始してください。** 「学びましょう」、「考えましょう」、「まとめ」セクションをグループで集まる前に完了します。

4. **グループで集まってください。** 毎週の集まりで、宿題を理解できたかどうか一緒に振り返ります。 「話し合いましょう」の質問を共に考え答えてください。

5. **「活かしましょう」セクションを完了してください。** グループで毎週の課題を確認します。 一緒に行うのが適切な課題と、個人で行う方が良い課題があります。

WEEK 1
第 1 週

THE CREATOR
創造主

WEEK 1
第 1 週

THE CREATOR
創造主

"In the beginning, God created the heavens and the earth..."
Genesis 1:1 (ESV)

「 はじめに神が天と地を創造された。」
創世記 1 章 1 節 (新改訳 2017)

THE CREATOR
創造主

God created the world and He created mankind. Each person is His artwork. He imagined and decided on the details of every plant and animal. He created the trees and designed the way the leaves fall. He gave birds their songs and wings they could use to fly. He made sunrises and sunsets. His creation is so incredible that only the greatest designer could have made it. God is the great designer of all things.

It is important to understand who God is as the Creator. We have a role as His created beings. We do not exist for ourselves or to serve ourselves. We exist to serve the One who created us. This is our purpose. Learning to live out His purpose in our lives is fulfilling, because we were designed to belong to Him.

神は世界を創造し、人類を創造されました。一人一人が神の作品です。神はすべての動植物の詳細を考えて定めました。神は森の中の木々を造り、葉がどのように落ちるかを設計されました。神は鳥たちに歌を与え、空を飛べる翼を与えました。神は日の出と日没を造りました。偉大なデザイナーにしか作ることができない、非常に素晴らしい創造です。　神はあらゆるものの偉大なデザイナーです。

神が創造主としてどの様な方かを理解することはとても重要です。私たちには神が創造してくださった存在としての役割があります。私たちは自分自身のためにも、自分自身に仕えるためにも存在していません。私たちを創造した方に仕えるために存在しているのです。これが私たちの生きる目的です。神の目的のために生きることを学ぶことは、私たちを満たしてくれます。なぜなら神に創造された者として、神のものとして生きるよう設計されているからです。

STUDY (学びましょう)

1. Read Genesis Chapter 1, and answer the following questions.
   創世記第 1 章を読んで、次の質問に答えてください。

   a. Who created the heavens and the earth? (Genesis 1:1)
      誰が天と地を創造しましたか？（創世記 1 章 1 節）

   b. Where did people come from? (Genesis 1:26-27)
      人々はどこから来ましたか？（創世記 1 章 26〜27 節）

2. What do the following verses explain about creation?
   次の聖句は創造について何を説明していますか？

   • Psalm 139:13-14 (詩篇 139 篇 13〜14 節)
     "For you formed my inward parts; you *knitted me together in my mother's womb. I praise you, for I am fearfully and wonderfully made. Wonderful are your works*; my soul knows it very well." (ESV)
     「あなたこそ　私の内臓を造り　母の胎の内で私を組み立てられた方です。私は感謝します。あなたは私に奇しいことをなさって恐ろしいほどです。私のたましいは　それをよく知っています。」 (新改訳 2017)

   • Hebrews 3:4 (ヘブル人への手紙 3 章 4 節)
     "For every house is built by someone, but *God is the builder of everything.*" (NIV)
     「家はそれぞれだれかが建てるのですが、すべてのものを造られたのは神です。」 (新改訳 2017)

3. What can we learn about our reason for existing from the following verses?
次の聖句から、私たちが存在する目的について、何を学ぶことができますか？

- 1 Corinthians 8:6 (コリント人への手紙第一 8 章 6 節)
"Yet for us there is one God, the Father, from whom are all things and *for whom we exist*, and one Lord, Jesus Christ, through whom are all things and through whom we exist." (ESV)
「私たちには、父なる唯一の神がおられるだけで、この神からすべてのものは発し、この神に私たちは至るからです。また、唯一の主なるイエスキリストがおられるだけで、この主によってすべてのものは存在し、この主によって私たちも存在するからです。」(新改訳 2017)

- Colossians 1:16 (コロサイ人への手紙 1 章 16 節)
"For by him all things were created, in heaven and on earth, visible and invisible, whether thrones or dominions or rulers or authorities — *all things were created through him and for him*." (ESV)
「なぜなら、天と地にあるすべてのものは、見えるものも見えないものも、王座であれ主権であれ、支配であれ権威であれ、御子にあって造られたからです。万物は御子によって造られ、御子のために造られました。」(新改訳 2017)

REFLECT (考えましょう)

1. The Bible tells us that God created the world and that He created people. Is this hard to believe? Why or why not?
聖書は、神が世界を創造されたこと、そして彼が人々を創造されたことを私たちに伝えています。これは信じがたいことですか？なぜ信じることができますか、または、なぜ信じられませんか？

2. What do you believe about where the world and people came from?
   あなたは世界と人々がどこから来たのかについて、何を信じていますか？

3. Romans 1:20 tells us that people are "without excuse" because the power of God has been clearly seen and understood through creation. When we look at a beautiful painting or a piece of pottery, we know that someone made it. If someone told us that it just appeared after billions of years, we might not believe them, because artwork looks too intentional to simply be a coincidence. In the same way, creation is too detailed to just be a coincidence. Our existence is not an accident. The magnificence of creation points to a creator. Does this comparison make you think differently about the creation story?

   ローマ人への手紙 1 章 20 節は、創造を通して創造する時から今までずっと神の力が明らかに見え、また理解することができるようになったので、人々は「弁解の余地がない」存在だと言っています。 美しい絵や陶器を見ると、誰かが作ったことがわかります。 数十万年後にただ突然現れたと誰かが言ったとしても、あまりにもその芸術作品が意図的に造られているように見えるため、単なる偶然なものとは信じないかもしれません。 創造についても同じです。 単なる偶然とするには、創造はあまりにも精密すぎます。創造の素晴らしさは、創造者がいることを示しています。 このような例えについて考えると、創造の物語が今までとは違うように感じますか？

4. How does it make you feel to know that God planned and designed you, and that you are wonderfully made?
   自分が神により計画され、また設計された「神の手作業」によりすばらしく造られた存在ということを知って、どのように感じますか？

<u>REVIEW</u> (まとめ)

God created the world and He created people. You were planned and designed by God and for God. We do not exist to serve ourselves. We exist to serve the One who created us.

神は世界を創造し、人間を創造しました。あなたは神によって、そして神のために計画され、設計されました。私たちは自分自身に仕えるために存在してはいません。私たちは私たちを創造してくださった方に仕えるために存在しています。

<u>DISCUSS</u> (話し合いましょう)

1. Do you have any questions about the reading or homework?
   読んだ箇所や宿題について何か質問がありますか？

2. What do you think about the creation story?
   創造の物語について、あなたはどう思っていますか？

3. Does knowing that God thought up and created the world make you appreciate it more?
   神が考え、この世を創造されたということを知ることで、より感謝の気持ちが生まれますか？

4. God created the world. He designed YOU. How does it make you feel to know you are one of God's creations?
   神は世を創造されました。彼はあなたをデザインしました。自分が神の創造物の1つであると理解することで、あなたはどう感じますか？

5. God created people for a purpose. Does it encourage you to know that the God of the universe has a purpose for you?
   神は目的を持って人々を造られました。あなたは天地の神があなたのために目的を持っていると知ることにより励まされますか？

6. What does Colossians 1:16 say about our purpose?
   コロサイ人への手紙1章16節は私たちの目的について何を語っていますか？

LIVE IT OUT (活かしましょう)

Go for a walk or hike this week. Look at the trees and animals and think about them as God's artwork. Look at the details in the way they look, move and the noises they make. God thought all of that up and created it!

今週、散歩に行ったりして、ハイキングに出かけてみましょう。木々や動物達を見て、それらが神の芸術作品であることを考えてみてください。それらの形や、動き、また出す音など、細かいところまで注意深くみてみましょう。神はそれらすべてを考え出し、創造されたのです！

NOTES (ノート)

WEEK 2
第 2 週

WHO IS GOD?
神は誰？

WEEK 2
第 2 週

WHO IS GOD?
神は誰？

"The Lord is good to all, and his mercy is over all that he has made."
Psalm 145:9 (ESV)

「主はすべてのものにいくつしみ深く
そのあわれみは　造られたすべてのものの上にあります。」
詩篇 145 篇 9 節 (新改訳 2017)

WHO IS GOD?
神は誰？

There is one God. He is all-powerful, all-knowing and ever-present. God is good. He loves us more than we can imagine. He is in control of everything. He is the Creator of all. Every breath we take is a gift from Him. The skills we have, and good health, are also gifts from Him. He has the power to give life and to take it away. He is a great healer. He is perfect, merciful, and just. He is our protector and comforter.

The Bible explains a lot about the character of God. Understanding more about how great, powerful, and loving He is can help people to trust and rely on Him. Even the greatest and most powerful person has limits, but God has no limits. Remember, again, that God created the world. He sustains all the life in the universe. He created everything from time and space down to the smallest atom. There is nothing He cannot do.

神は唯一です。神は全力であり、全知全能であり遍在（空間の中にどこにでも存在すること）している方です。神は良い方です。神は私たちの想像以上に私たちを愛しておられます。神はすべてをコントロールしています。神はすべての創造主です。私たちの呼吸一つ一つが、神からの贈り物です。 私たちのスキル、健康も贈り物です。 彼には命を与え、また取り去る力があります。神は素晴らしい癒しを与えてくださる方です。完全で、憐れみ深く、公正な方です。神は私たちを守る方であり、慰めを与えてくださいます。

聖書は神の性格について多くを説明しています。神がどれほど偉大で、力強く、また愛情深い方であるかを深く理解することは、神を信じ、頼ることの手助けとなります。この世で最も偉大で力ある人でさえも限界がありますが、神には限界がありません。繰り返し言いますが、神が世界を創造したことを覚えておいてください。神は天地のすべての生命を支えています。神は時間と空間から最小の原子に至るまで、すべてを創造されました。彼にできないことは何もありません。

__STUDY__ (学びましょう)

1. We can learn more about God from the Bible. What do the verses below say about God?
    聖書から神についてさらに学ぶことができます。次の聖句は神について何を語っていますか？

    *   Exodus 34:6-7 (出エジプト記 34 章 6〜7 節)
        "And he passed in front of Moses, proclaiming, 'The Lord, the Lord, the *compassionate and gracious God, slow to anger, abounding in love and faithfulness, maintaining love to thousands, and forgiving wickedness, rebellion and sin...'*" (NIV)
        「__主__は彼の前を通り過ぎるとき、こう宣言された。「__主__、__主__は、あわれみ深く、情け深い神。怒るのに遅く、恵みとまことに富み、恵みを千代まで保ち、咎と背きと罪を赦す。...」 (新改訳 2017)

    *   Deuteronomy 10:17-18 (申命記 10 章 17〜18 節)
        "For the Lord your God is God of gods and Lord of lords, the great God, mighty and awesome, who *shows no partiality and accepts no bribes. He defends the cause of the fatherless and the widow, and loves the foreigner residing among you*, giving them food and clothing." (NIV)
        「あなたがたの神、__主__は神の神、主の主、偉大で力があり、恐ろしい神。えこひいきをせず、賄賂を取らず、みなしごや、やもめのためにさばきを行い、寄留者を愛して、これに食物と衣服を与えられる。 (新改訳 2017)

    *   Isaiah 6:3 (イザヤ書 6 章 3 節)
        "And they were calling to one another: '*Holy, holy, holy is the Lord Almighty; the whole earth is full of his glory.*'" (NIV)
        「互いにこう呼び交わしていた。「聖なる、聖なる、聖なる、万軍の__主__。その栄光は全地に満ちる。」」 (新改訳 2017)

2. God is omnipresent and all-powerful. What do the following verses show us about His power and abilities?
神は遍在で強い方です。次の聖句は神の力と能力ついてどの何を語っていますか？

- Hebrews 4:13 (ヘブル人への手紙 4 章 13 節)
  "Nothing in all creation is hidden from God's sight. Everything is uncovered and laid bare before the eyes of him to whom we must give account." (NIV)
  「神の御前にあらわでない被造物はありません。神の目にはすべてが裸であり、さらけ出されています。この神に対して、私たちは申し開きをするのです。 (新改訳 2017)

- Revelation 3:7 (ヨハネの黙示録 3 章 7 節)
  "...What he opens no one can shut, and what he shuts no one can open." (NIV)
  「...彼が開くと、だれも閉じることがなく、彼が閉じると、だれも開くことがない...」 (新改訳 2017)

- Job 12:10 (ヨブ記 12 章 10 節)
  "In his hand is the life of every living thing and the breath of all mankind." (ESV)
  「すべての生き物のいのちと、すべての肉なる人の息は、その御手のうちにある。」 (新改訳 2017)

- Psalm 145:15-16 (詩篇 145 篇 15〜16 節)
  "The eyes of all look to you, and you give them their food at the proper time. You open your hand and satisfy the desires of every living thing." (NIV)
  「すべての目はあなたを待ち望んでいます。あなたは　時にかなって彼らに食物を与えられます。あなたは御手を開き生けるものすべての願いを満たされます。」 (新改訳 2017)

3. God loves people so much. What do the following verses say about God's love?
神は人々をとても愛しています。次の聖句は、神の愛について何を語っていますか？

- 1 John 4:7-8 (ヨハネの手紙第一 4 章 7〜8 節)
"Beloved, let us love one another, for *love is from God*, and whoever loves has been born of God and knows God. Anyone who does not love does not know God, because *God is love.*" (ESV)
「愛する者たち。私たちは互いに愛し合いましょう。愛は神から出ているのです。愛があるものはみな神から生まれ、神を知っています。愛のない者は神を知りません。神は愛だからです。」(新改訳 2017)

- Romans 5:8 (ローマ人への手紙 5 章 8 節)
"But God demonstrates his own love for us in this: *While we were still sinners, Christ died for us.*" (NIV)
「しかし、私たちがまだ罪人であったとき、キリストが私たちのために死なれたことによって、神は私たちに対するご自分の愛を明らかにしておられます。(新改訳 2017)

- James 1:17 (ヤコブの手紙 1 章 17 節)
"*Every good and perfect gift is from above*, coming down from the Father of the heavenly lights, who does not change like shifting shadows." (NIV)
「すべての良い贈り物、またすべての完全な賜物は上からのものであり、光を造られた父から下ってくるのです。父には、移り変わりや、天体の運行によって生じる影のようなものはありません。」 (新改訳 2017)

4. God gives special promises to those who choose to follow Him. What promises are found in these verses?
神は神に従うことを選ぶ人々に特別な約束を与えます。次の聖句には何を約束していますか？

- Joshua 1:9 (ヨシュア記 1 章 9 節)
  "Have I not commanded you? Be strong and courageous. Do not be afraid; do not be discouraged, for the Lord *your God will be with you wherever you go.*" (NIV)
  「わたしはあなたに命じたではないか。強くあれ。雄々しくあれ。恐れてはならない。おののいてはならない。あなたが行くところどこででも、あなたの神、主があなたとともにおられるのだから。」(新改訳 2017)

- Romans 8:28 (ローマ人への手紙 8 章 28 節)
  "And we know that in all things *God works for the good of those who love him*, who have been called according to his purpose." (NIV)
  「神を愛する人たち、すなわち、神のご計画にしたがって召された人たちのためには、すべてのことがともに働いて益となることを、私たちは知っています。」(新改訳 2017)

- Matthew 11:28 (マタイによる福音書 11 章 28 節)
  "Come to me, all you who are weary and burdened, and *I will give you rest.*"
  「すべて疲れた人、重荷を負っている人はわたしのもとに来なさい。わたしがあなたがたを休ませてあげます。」(新改訳 2017)

- Psalm 46:1 (詩篇 46 篇 1 節)
  "God is *our refuge and strength*, a very present *help in trouble.*" (ESV)
  「神は　われらの避け所　また力。苦しむとき　そこにある強き助け。
  (新改訳 2017)

REFLECT (考えましょう)

1. What have you learned about God from the reading so far?
   ここまで読んだ箇所から神について何を学びましたか？

2. What impresses you the most about God's character?
   神の性格について最も印象に残っていることは何ですか？

3. Read Luke 15:11-32. God's love for us is like this father's love for his son. How does this make you feel?
   ルカの福音書 15 章 11〜32 節を読みましょう。私たちに対する神の愛は、父親の息子に対する愛のようなものです。そのことについてあなたはどう感じますか？

REVIEW (まとめ)

God is holy, yet compassionate. He is just, but also generous, gracious, and merciful. He is our defender, protector, and refuge. He provides for our needs and sustains our every breath. God loves us. He is the giver of all good gifts. We cannot ignore God's care or His saving hand upon us. We have an utter dependence on Him. God is completely in control, and we live because of His continual provision and sustainment.

神は聖なるものでありながら、慈悲深い方です。 彼は公正な方であると同時に、寛大で、恵み深くまた慈悲深い方です。 彼は私たちの擁護者、保護者であり避け所です。 私たちのニーズを満たし、私たちの一つ一つの呼吸を維持しているのは神です。 神は私たちを愛しています。 すべての良い贈り物を与えてくださるのは神です。 神の気遣いや救いの手を無視することはできません。私たちは神に完全に依存しています。神が完全に支配し、絶え間なく支えてくださっているからこそ私たちは生きているのです。

DISCUSS (話し合いましょう)

1. Do you have any questions about the reading or homework?
   読んだ箇所や宿題について何か質問がありますか？

2. What does the Bible tell us about God?
   聖書は神について私たちに何を語っていますか？

3. What do you admire about God?
   神のどの点について感嘆しますか？

4. Read Luke 15:11-32. God loves us like this father loved his son. What did you think about this story?
   ルカの福音書 15 章 11〜32 節を読んでください。この父が息子を愛したように、神は私たちを愛してくださっています。この話についてどう思いましたか？

5. Have you ever seen an example of mercy and forgiveness like the one in Luke 15:11-32?
   ルカの福音書 15 章 11〜32 節のような憐れみと赦しの実例を今までみたことがありますか？

6. God will forgive us too when we ask for it in our prayers. Is there anything you would like to ask God to forgive you for today?
   祈りの中で私たちが赦しを求めると、神も私たちを赦してくださいます。今日神に赦して欲しいことはありますか？

LIVE IT OUT (活かしましょう)

Pray to the God of the Bible this week. Talk to Him like you would talk to a friend or family member. Thank Him for being a loving God. Share your concerns with Him. Listen to Him. You can pray anywhere and anytime. You are not limited to praying in a specific way. God wants us to talk to Him and listen to Him. He wants to have a relationship with you.

今週、聖書が語っている神に祈ってください。友人や家族と会話するように、神と話してみてください。神が愛の方であることを感謝しましょう。あなたの懸念していることを共有してください。神が語ることに耳を傾けましょう。祈ることは、いつでもどこでもできます。特定の方法で祈る必要はありません。神は、私たちに話してもらいたい、また神の言葉に耳を傾けてほしいと思っていらっしゃいます。神はあなたと交わりを持ちたいのです。

NOTES (ノート)

WEEK 3
第 3 週

THE PROBLEM OF SIN
罪の問題

THE PROBLEM OF SIN
罪の問題

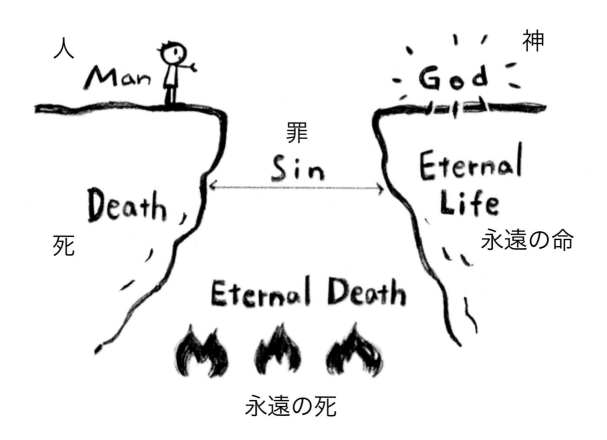

"...all have sinned and fall short of the glory of God."
Romans 3:23 (ESV)

「すべての人は罪を犯して、神の栄光を受けることができず、」
ローマ人への手紙 3 章 23 節 (新改訳 2017)

THE PROBLEM OF SIN
罪の問題

In the beginning, man was separated from God because of wrongs he committed against God. The first two people, Adam and Eve, disobeyed God. The punishment for this sin was death. No amount of good works could fix the relationship. We still sin against God today too. Sin is not just a bad crime that you can go to jail for. Lying, cheating, impatience, selfishness and being unloving or unkind toward others are all sins. The relationship with God was broken because of our sin. God is holy and perfect, and nothing contaminated by sin can remain in His presence.

Remember, God loves people very much. He created and designed us. He did not want people to stay separated from Him. He sent His Son Jesus down to earth to rescue all who believe in Him from the punishment of death. This gift of reconciliation and salvation is very precious. Before we can truly understand how meaningful this gift is, we must first understand the sin and consequences that we have been saved from.

はじめに、神に対して間違ったことを行ったために、人間は神から引き離されました。人類最初の二人であるアダムとエバは、神に従いませんでした。この罪に対する罰は死です。良い行いをどんなにしても、神との関係を修正することはできません。私たちは今日に至っても神に対して罪を犯しています。罪は、刑務所に行かなければならないような悪い犯罪だけを指している訳ではありません。嘘、ごまかし、苛立ち、わがままであること、他人を愛さないこと、または不親切であることなど、すべて罪です。神と私たちとの関係は、私たちの罪が原因で壊れました。神は聖く完全であり、罪によって汚れたものは全て神と同じ場所にいることができません。

神は人をとても愛していることを思い出してください。彼は私たちを造り、デザインされました。神は人々が神ご自身から離れたままでいることを望みませんでした。神は息子イエスをこの世に遣わされ、彼を信じるすべての人を死の罰から救いました。和解と救いは、非常に貴重な贈り物です。この贈り物がどれほど大事な意味を持つものであるかを真に理解するためには、神が救ってくださった私たちの罪とその結果についてまず理解しなければなりません。

<u>STUDY</u> (学びましょう)

1. Read Genesis Chapters 2 and 3, which tell the story of "original sin." This single act of disobedience resulted in severe punishment.
「原罪」について論じている創世記第 2、3 章を読んでください。このたった一つの不従順な行為が、厳しい罰をもたらしました。

    a. What did God tell Adam NOT to do? (Genesis 2:16-17)
神はアダムに禁止したことは何でしたか？（創世記 2 章 16〜17 節）

    b. What did Adam and Eve do in Genesis 3:1-6?
アダムとエバは創世記第 3 章 1〜6 節で何をしましたか？

    c. What was the punishment for their disobedience? (Genesis 3:16-19)
彼らの不従順に対する罰は何でしたか？（創世記 3 章 16〜19 節）

    d. How did this affect their relationship with God? (Genesis 3:23)
これは神との関係にどんな影響を与えましたか？（創世記 3 章 23 節）

    e. What did God provide after Adam and Eve had sinned? He still took care of and loved His people, even after they disobeyed Him. (Genesis 3:21)
アダムとエバが罪を犯した後、神は何を与えましたか？ 神は、彼らが従わなかった後も、ご自分の民を大事にし、愛していました。
（創世記 3 章 21 節）

2. The Bible discusses many types of sin against God. What sins do these verses mention?
聖書は、神に対する様々な罪について語っています。次の聖句はどんな罪を言及していますか？

- Galatians 5:19-21 (ガラテヤの信徒への手紙 5 章 19〜21 節)
  "The acts of the flesh are obvious: *sexual immorality, impurity and debauchery; idolatry and witchcraft; hatred, discord, jealousy, fits of rage, selfish ambition, dissensions, factions and envy; drunkenness, orgies, and the like*. I warn you, as I did before, that those who live like this will not inherit the kingdom of God." (NIV)
  「肉のわざは明らかです。すなわち、淫らな行い、汚れ、好色、偶像礼拝、魔術、敵意、争い、そねみ、憤り、党派心、分裂、分派、ねたみ、泥酔、遊興、そういった類のものです。以前にも言ったように、今もあなたがたにあらかじめ言っておきます。このようなことをしている者たちは神の国を相続できません。」(新改訳 2017)

- Mark 7:20-23 (マルコの福音書 7 章 20〜23 節)
  "And he said, 'What comes out of a person is what defiles him. For from within, out of the heart of man, come *evil thoughts, sexual immorality, theft, murder, adultery, coveting, wickedness, deceit, sensuality, envy, slander, pride, foolishness*. All these evil things come from within, and they defile a person.'" (ESV)
  「イエスはまた言われた。「人から出て来るもの、それが人を汚すのです。内側から、すなわち人の心の中から、悪い考えが出て来ます。淫らな行い、盗み、殺人、姦淫、貪欲、悪行、欺き、好色、ねたみ、ののしり、高慢、愚かさで、これらの悪は、みな内側から出て来て、人を汚すのです。」」(新改訳 2017)

- James 4:17 (ヤコブの手紙 4 章 17 節)
  "So, whoever *knows the right thing to do and fails to do it*, for him it is sin." (ESV)
  「こういうわけで、なすべき良いことを知っていながら行わないなら、それはその人には罪です。」(新改訳 2017)

3. Who is guilty of sin against God, according to Romans 3:23?
ローマ人への手紙 3 章 23 節によると、だれが神に対して罪を犯しましたか？

"…all have sinned and fall short of the glory of God." (ESV)
「すべての人は罪を犯して、神の栄光を受けることができず、」(新改訳 2017)

4. What are the consequences of sin mentioned in these verses?
これらの聖句で述べられている罪の結果とは何ですか？

- Romans 6:23 (ローマ人への手紙 6 章 23 節)
  "For the *wages of sin is death*, but the free gift of God is eternal life in Christ Jesus our Lord." (ESV)
  「罪の報酬は死です。しかし神の賜物は、私たちの主キリスト・イエスにある永遠のいのちです。」(新改訳 2017)

- Romans 5:12 (ローマ人への手紙 5 章 12 節)
  "Therefore, just as sin came into the world through one man, and death through sin, and *so death spread to all men because all sinned—*" (ESV)
  「こういうわけで、ちょうど一人の人によって罪が世界に入り、罪によって死が入り、こうして、すべての人が罪を犯したので、死がすべての人に広がったのと同様に―」(新改訳 2017)

- Isaiah 59:2 (イザヤ書 59 章 2 節)
  "But your iniquities have made a *separation between you and your God*, and your sins have hidden his face from you so that he does not hear." (ESV)
  「むしろ、あなたがたの咎が、あなたがたと、あなたがたの神との仕切りとなり、あなたがたの罪が御顔を隠させ、聞いてくださらないようにしたのだ。」(新改訳 2017)

5. Read the "Ten Commandments" in Exodus 20:1-17. These are laws that God gave to His people. In the New Testament, Jesus taught that even thinking about doing some of these things is a sin. Are any of these commandments difficult to obey?
出エジプト記 20 章 1〜17 節の「十戒」を読みましょう。これらは神が神の民に与えた律法です。新約聖書では、イエスはこれらの行いについて考えるだけでも罪であると教えられました。これらの戒めに従うことは難しいですか？

6. John 3:16 explains the way to salvation from the punishment of sin and death. How can we get this salvation?
ヨハネの福音書 3 章 16 節は、罪と死の罰からの救いの道を説明しています。私たちはどのように、この救いを得ることができますか？

"For God so loved the world, that he gave his only Son, that whoever believes in him should not perish but have eternal life." (ESV)
「神は、実に、そのひとり子をお与えになったほどに世を愛された。それは御子を信じる者が、一人として滅びることなく、永遠のいのちを持つためである。」
(新改訳 2017)

7. Who is "the Son" from John 3:16 that can save us?
ヨハネの福音書 3 章 16 節によると、私たちを救うことのできる「子」は誰ですか？

REFLECT (考えましょう)

1. What did you learn about sin from this chapter?
    この章で罪について何を学びましたか？

2. God offers forgiveness from sin. After reading about what sin is, do you believe you need His forgiveness?
    神は罪からの赦しを差し伸べています。罪とは何かを読んだ後、あなたは神の赦しが必要だと思いますか？

3. 1 John 1:9 teaches those who believe to confess their sins to the Lord. When believers repent and confess their wrongs to Him, He will forgive them and cleanse them of unrighteousness. Is there anything you would like to ask Him to forgive you for?
    ヨハネの手紙第一 1 章 9 節は、信じる者は自分の罪を主に告白するよう教えています。信じる者が悔い改め、自分の過ちを彼に告白すると、彼は私たちを赦し、不義を清めます。彼に赦しをお願いしたいことはありますか？

    "If we confess our sins, he is faithful and just to forgive us our sins and to cleanse us from all unrighteousness." (ESV)
    「もし私たちが自分の罪を告白するなら、神は真実で正しい方ですから、その罪を赦し、私たちをすべての不義からきよめてくださいます。」(新改訳 2017)

REVIEW (まとめ)

Sin is disobedience against God. Even small acts of disobedience against Him are sinful. The punishment for sin is death. There is separation between God and man, because of sin. We cannot escape the consequence of sin by doing good works. God offers salvation only through His Son Jesus Christ.

罪は神に対する不従順です。神に対する小さな不従順な行為でさえも罪深いのです。罪に対する罰は死です。罪が原因で、神と人の間には隔たりがあります。 善い行いによっても罪の結果から逃れることはできません。 神は御子イエス・キリストを通してのみ救いを提供されます。

DISCUSS (話し合いましょう)

1. Do you have any questions about the reading or homework?
   読んだ箇所や宿題について何か質問がありますか？

2. What are some examples of sin?
   罪の具体例は何ですか？

3. Sin is not just a big crime. Lying, impatience, selfishness and harshness toward others are all sins. Have you ever done any of these things?
   大きな犯罪だけが罪ではありません。嘘、苛立ち、わがまま、他の人に対して辛くあたることなど、すべて罪です。あなたはこれらのことをした経験がありますか？

4. What does Romans 6:23 tell us the consequence of our sin is?
   ローマ人への手紙 6 章 23 節には、私たちの罪の結果が何であると書かれていますか？

5. What hope is there in the second half of Romans 6:23?
   ローマ人への手紙 6 章 23 節の聖句の後半にはどの希望が書かれていますか？

6. Do you know who Jesus is and what He came to do?
   あなたはイエスが誰であるか、そして何のために来られたか知っていますか？

LIVE IT OUT (活かしましょう)

Think about any areas in your life where you have sinned. Do not be discouraged by it. Seek forgiveness for it. God does not want you to walk in shame. He wants to forgive you. He wants to lift you back up into a relationship with Him. He is generous and gracious. Just confess your sins to Him, and He will forgive you. This is possible because of the sacrifice that Jesus made by dying on the cross for us. When you choose to believe in Jesus and repent of your sin, you will be forgiven.

あなたの人生の中で犯した罪について考えて見てください。それに捉われて落胆しないでください。その罪に対する赦しを求めてください。神はあなたが恥と共に生きていくことを望まず、あなたを赦したいのです。神はあなたとの関係を取り戻したいと思っています。神は寛大で恵み深い方です。あなたの罪を神に告白するだけで、神はあなたを赦してくださいます。イエスが生贄として、死んでくださったことにより、それが可能となったのです。イエスを信じて罪を悔い改める決断をする時、あなたは赦されます。

NOTES (ノート)

WEEK 4
第４週

SALVATION
救い

WEEK 4
第4週

SALVATION
救い

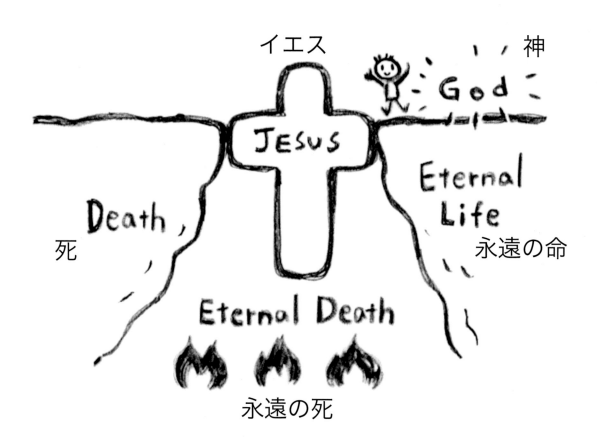

"For God so loved the world that he gave his one and only Son,
that whoever believes in him shall not perish but have eternal life."
John 3:16 (NIV)

「神は、実に、そのひとり子をお与えになったほどに世を愛された。
それは御子が信じる者が、一人として滅びることなく、
永遠のいのちを持つためである。」
ヨハネの福音書3章16節 (新改訳 2017)

SALVATION
救い

Jesus came down to earth to rescue us from sin and death. Jesus is the Son of God, and He is also God. He is fully God and fully man. He has all authority in heaven and on earth. While He was on earth, He did many miracles. He healed people and shared wise messages. Many people followed Him. He was perfect and never sinned.

Jesus was accused of crimes He did not commit. He was arrested and crucified (put to death on the cross). After three days, He rose again. He ascended to heaven and He is alive today. He sent the Holy Spirit to be with us, so that we could have a relationship with God.

He faced the punishment of death for all of mankind and had victory over it, so that we could be free. He conquered death and defeated sin. We have all sinned and deserve the punishment of death, but Jesus took our place and paid the price for our sins. He chose to lay down His life, offering it in exchange for ours and rescuing us from the grave. Only a perfect sacrifice could atone for sin once and for all.

He offers this salvation to all who believe in Him. We can now be reconciled to God through His Son. We celebrate Easter in remembrance of His death and resurrection.

イエスは私たちを罪と死から救い出すためにこの世に来られました。 イエスは神の子であり、また神でもあります。 完全に神であり、また同時に完全に人間でもありました。イエスは天と地のすべての権威を持っています。イエスはこの地にいる間、多くの奇跡を起こしました。 人々を癒し、知恵に満ちた言葉を人々に話しました。 多くの人がイエスに従いました。イエスは完全で決して罪を犯しませんでした。

イエスは犯していない罪に問われました。イエスは逮捕され、十字架につけられて死にました。 そして 3 日後によみがえりました。イエスは天に昇り、今も生きています。私たちが神と交わりを持てるよう、聖霊を私たちに送られ、共におられます。

イエスは私たちを解放するため、すべての人類の死の罰を受け、それに勝利しました。彼は死を征服し罪を打ち負かしました。私たちは罪を犯し、死の罰に価しますが、イエスが私たちの代わりにその罰を受け罪の代価を支払ってくださいました。イエスは私たちを墓から救うために、ご自身の命と私たちの命と引き換えに捧げることを選ばれました。完全な犠牲だけが、一度に罪を完全に償うことができました。

彼を信じる者すべてにこの救いを差し伸べています。今私たちは神の子を通じて神と和解することができます。私たちは イエスの死と復活を記念して、イースター（復活祭）を祝います。

STUDY (学びましょう)

1. Read through the following passages from the Book of Mark. What happened in each of these sections and what do they tell you about Jesus?
   マルコの福音書から次の聖句を読んでください。 それぞれの聖句で何が起こりましたか？またイエスについて何を語っていますか？

   - Mark 1:21-34 (マルコの福音書 1 章 21〜34 節)

   - Mark 4:35-41 (マルコの福音書 4 章 35〜41 節)

   - Mark 5:1-20 (マルコの福音書 5 章 1〜20 節)

   - Mark 5:21-43 (マルコの福音書 5 章 21〜43 節)

   - Mark 14:12-72 (マルコの福音書 14 章 12〜72 節)

   - Mark 15:1 – Mark 16:8 (マルコの福音書 15 章 1 節 〜 16 章 8 節)

2. What do the following verses tell us about Jesus?
次の聖句は、イエスについて何を語っていますか？

- Matthew 28:18 (マタイ の福音書 28 章 18 節)
  "And Jesus came and said to them, '*All authority in heaven and on earth* has been given to me.'" (ESV)
  「イエスは近づいて来て、彼らにこう言われた。「わたしは天においても地においても、すべての権威が与えられています。」」(新改訳 2017)

- 1 Timothy 2:5-6 (テモテへの手紙第一 2 章 5〜6 節)
  "For there is one God, and there is *one mediator* between God and men, the man Christ Jesus, who *gave himself as a ransom for all*, which is the testimony given at the proper time." (ESV)
  「神は唯一です。神と人との間の仲介者も唯一であり、それは人としてのキリスト・イエスです。キリストは、すべての人の贖いの代価として、ご自分を与えてくださいました。これは、定められた時になされた証です。」
  (新改訳 2017)

- John 1:18 (ヨハネの福音書 1 章 18 節)
  "No one has ever seen God, but *the one and only Son, who is himself God* and is in closest relationship with the Father, has made him known." (NIV)
  「いまだかつて神を見た者はいない。父のふところにおられるひとり子の神が、神を解き明かされたのである。」(新改訳 2017)

- John 10:30 (ヨハネの福音書 10 章 30 節)
  "I and the Father are one." (ESV)
  「わたしと父とは一つです。」(新改訳 2017)

3. What do the following verses tell us about salvation?
   次の聖句は、救いについて何を語っていますか？

   - Romans 10:9 (ローマ人への手紙 10 章 9 節)
     "...if you *confess with your mouth that Jesus is Lord* and *believe in your heart that God raised him from the dead,* you will be saved." (ESV)
     「...もしあなたの口でイエスを主と告白し、あなたの心で神はイエスを死者の中からよみがえらせたと信じるなら、あなたは救われるからです。」
     (新改訳 2017)

   - Mark 16:16 (マルコの福音書 16 章 16 節)
     "Whoever believes and is baptized will be saved, but whoever does not believe will be condemned." (ESV)
     「信じてバプテスマを受ける者は救われます。しかし、信じない者は罪に定められます。」(新改訳 2017)

   - John 3:16 (ヨハネの福音書 3 章 16 節)
     "For God so loved the world, that he *gave his only Son,* that *whoever believes* in him *should not perish* but have eternal life." (ESV)
     「神は、実に、そのひとり子をお与えになったほどに世を愛された。それは御子を信じる者が、一人として滅びることなく、永遠のいのちを持つためである。」((新改訳 2017)

   - John 14:6 (ヨハネの福音書 14 章 6 節)
     "Jesus said to him, 'I am *the way, and the truth, and the life.* No one comes to the Father except through me.'" (ESV)
     「イエスは彼に言われた。「わたしが道であり、真理であり、いのちなのです。わたしを通してでなければ、だれも父のみもとに行くことはできません。」(新改訳 2017)

REFLECT (考えましょう)

1. Who is Jesus?
   イエスは誰ですか？

2. Mark, Chapters 15:1-16:20, summarizes the story of Jesus' death and resurrection. How did it make you feel to read through His story?
   マルコの福音書 15 章 1 節〜16 章 20 節は、イエスの死と復活の物語を要約しています。 彼の物語を読んでどう感じましたか？

3. Why did Jesus give His life for us on the cross? (John 3:16)
   なぜ、イエスは十字架で私たちのために命を与えられたのですか？
   (ヨハネの福音書 3 章 16 節)

4. What happened to Jesus after He died? (Acts 5:30; Mark 16:6-8)
   イエスが死んだ後に、イエスはどうなりましたか？
   (使徒の働き 5 章 30 節、マルコの福音書 16 章 6〜8 節)

5. Do you want the free gift of salvation that God offers through Jesus?
   あなたは、神がイエスを通して与えてくださる無償の贈り物である救いが欲しいですか？

REVIEW (まとめ)

Jesus is the Savior of the world. He is God, who came down as man, to save mankind from sin and death. When you believe in Him, you can receive forgiveness and the gift of eternal life. Jesus came to earth because God loves us and wants to have a relationship with us.

イエスは世界の救い主です。この方は人類を罪と死から救うために人間として降りてきて下さった神です。あなたが彼を信じるとき、あなたは赦しと永遠の命の贈り物を受け取ることができます。イエスが地上に来られたのは、神が私たちを愛しており、私たちと交わりを持ちたいからです。

DISCUSS (話し合いましょう)

1. Do you have any questions about the reading or homework?
   読んだ箇所や宿題について何か質問がありますか？

2. What did Jesus do for mankind?
   イエスは人類のために何をしましたか？

3. What do you think about Jesus and the gift of salvation that He offers to us?
   イエスのことについて、また、彼が私たちに与えてくださる救いの贈り物についてどう思いますか？

4. Do you know anyone who would give up their life for you?
   あなたのために、自分の命を断つ人を知っていますか？

5. Jesus told His disciples exactly what was going to happen to Him, and then it did. They still had trouble believing Him, even though He did many miracles right in front of them. Do you have trouble believing in Him?
   イエスは弟子たちに、彼にこれから何が起きるかを正確に告げ、それが実際に起こりました。彼が弟子たちの前で多くの奇跡が行われたにもかかわらず、弟子たちはまだイエスをなかなか信じることができませんでした。あなたはイエスを信じるのに難しさを感じていますか？

6. Salvation is a free gift from the Lord. Do you want to receive salvation today and start having a relationship with Jesus?
   救いは主からの無償の贈り物です。あなたは今日救いを受けとって、イエスとの交わりを持ち始めたいですか？

LIVE IT OUT (活かしましょう)

Would you like to receive Jesus Christ as your Lord and Savior today? If so, go to the Lord and ask for His forgiveness. Repent and choose to believe the gospel. If you are not sure how to start, you can pray the prayer below with your small group leader or during your prayer time at home:

"I believe that Jesus is Lord and that God raised Him from the dead. I believe that if I confess my sins, that God will forgive my sins. Lord, I am sorry for my sins against you. Please forgive me and save me. Please help me to live a life that is pleasing to you. In Jesus name, amen."

This is the beginning of your new life with the Lord. Thank Him for saving you from sin and death. If you still have trouble believing, pray and ask God to help you believe. Keep reading through the Bible and practicing what it teaches, and you will see the truth in it.

Reference verses: Romans 10:9; 1 John 1:9

　今日、あなたはイエス・キリストを主であり救い主として受け入れたいですか？もしそうなら、主の元に行き、主の赦しを求めてください。 悔い改め、福音を信じることを選んでください。 どのように始めれば良いのかわからない場合は、グループリーダーと一緒に、または自宅での祈りの時間中に、以下のように祈ることができます。

　「イエスは主であり、神は彼を死からよみがえらせたと信じます。私は自分の罪を告白すれば、神は私の罪を赦してくださると信じます。主よ、あなたに対して罪を犯したことを赦し、私を救ってください。あなたの喜ばれる人生を送れるように助けて下さい。イエスの御名において祈ります、アーメン。」

　これが主との新しい人生の始まりです。罪と死からあなたを救った神に感謝します。それでもまだ信じられない場合は、神に信じられるように神の助けを祈り求めてください。聖書を読み続け、聖書が教えていることを実践してください。そうすれば、聖書の真実を見ることができます。

　参照聖句：ローマ人への手紙 10 章 9 節、 ヨハネの手紙第一　1 章 9 節

NOTES (ノート)

WEEK 4

WEEK 5
第 5 週

WHAT IS
ETERNAL LIFE?
永遠の命とは？

WEEK 5
第 5 週

WHAT IS ETERNAL LIFE?
永遠の命とは？

"He will wipe away every tear from their eyes, and *death shall be no more,*
neither shall there be mourning, nor crying, nor pain anymore,
for the former things have passed away."
Revelation 21:4 (ESV)

「神は彼らの目から涙をことごとくぬぐい取ってくださる。
もはや死はなく、悲しみも、叫び声も、苦しみもない。
以前のものが過ぎ去ったからである。」
ヨハネの黙示録 21 章 4 節 (新改訳 2017)

WHAT IS ETERNAL LIFE?
永遠の命とは？

When we die, we face judgment before God for everything we have ever done. Even our thoughts and our words will be judged. Those who are judged righteous will go to heaven and live with God forever. This is eternal life. Heaven is a beautiful, peaceful place.

Those who are judged unrighteous will be cast into the lake of fire. This is a place for the dead, apart from God, with great pain and suffering. The lake of fire is the second death. The first death that people face is the physical death of the body, which humanity continues to face. The second death is a spiritual death of the soul.

All people who sin against God and do not repent will face the second death. Jesus saves and spares those who believe in Him from the second death. He gives them eternal life and makes them righteous. They remain alive in spirit and receive new bodies at the return of Christ.

私たちが死ぬとき、私たちは神の前で今までしてきたことすべてについての裁きに直面します。私たちの考えや言葉さえも裁かれます。義と判断された人は天国に行き、神と共に永遠に生きます。これが永遠の命です。天国は美しく平和な場所です。

不義と判断された者は火の池に投げ込まれることになります。これは、大きな痛みと苦しみのある場所、神と離れた死者のための場所です。火の池が２番目の死です。最初の死は肉体の物理的な死であり、人類はこれに直面し続けます。２番目の死は魂の霊的な死です。

神に罪を犯し、悔い改めない人は全て、魂の霊的な死である第二の死に直面します。イエスは自分を信じる人々を救い、第二の死から解放します。イエスは彼らに永遠の命を与え義とされます。彼らは霊において生き続け、イエス・キリストが戻られた時に新しい体を受け取ります。

STUDY (学びましょう)

1. The Book of Revelation is a mysterious prophetic account of the end times and life after death. What can you learn from the following sections about life after death?
ヨハネの黙示録は、終わりの時と死後の人生についての神秘的で預言的な書です。あなたは死後の生活について次の聖句から何を学ぶことができますか?

   - Revelation 20:11-15 (ヨハネの黙示録 20 章 11〜15 節)

   - Revelation 21:1-8 (ヨハネの黙示録 21 章 1〜8 節)

2. What does Revelation 21:8 tell us will happen to people who do not believe in Jesus?
ヨハネの黙示録 21 章 8 節は、イエスを信じていない人々に何が起こると教えていますか?

3. In John 5:24, Jesus tells us the way to escape judgment and gain eternal life. What is it?
ヨハネの福音書第 5 章 24 節で、イエスは裁きを免れて永遠の命を得るための道を私たちに語っています。それは何ですか?

   "Truly, truly, I say to you, *whoever hears my word and believes him who sent me has eternal life*. He does not come into judgment but has passed from death to life." (ESV)
   「まことに、まことに、あなたがたに言います。わたしのことばを聞いて、わたしを遣わされた方を信じる者は、永遠の命を持ち、さばきにあうことがなく、死からいのちに移っています。」(新改訳 2017)

4. When we listen to the word of Jesus and believe, we are set free from judgment and gain eternal life. What do the following passages reveal about eternal life?
イエスの言葉に耳を傾けて信じた時に、私たちは裁きから解放され永遠の命を得ます。次の聖句は、永遠の命について何を明らかにしていますか？

- Revelation 21:4 (ヨハネの黙示録 21 章 4 節)
  "*He will wipe away every tear from their eyes, and death shall be no more, neither shall there be mourning, nor crying, nor pain anymore,* for the former things have passed away." (ESV)
  「神は彼らの目から涙をことごとくぬぐい取ってくださる。もはや死はなく、悲しみも、叫び声も、苦しみもない。以前のものが過ぎ去ったからである」
  (新改訳 2017)

- Philippians 3:20-21 (ピリピ人への手紙 3 章 20〜21 節)
  "But our *citizenship is in heaven.* And we eagerly await a Savior from there, the Lord Jesus Christ, who, by the power that enables him to bring everything under his control, will *transform our lowly bodies so that they will be like his glorious body.*" (NIV)
  「しかし、私たちの国籍は天にあります。そこから主イエス・キリストが救い主として来られるのを、私たちは待ち望んでいます。キリストは、万物をご自分に従わせることさえできる御力によって、私たちの卑しいからだを、ご自分の栄光に輝くからだと同じ姿に変えてくださいます。」 (新改訳 2017)

- John 14:2-3 (ヨハネの福音書 14 章 2〜3 節)
  "*My Father's house* has many rooms; if that were not so, would I have told you that I am going there to *prepare a place for you*? And if I go and prepare a place for you, I will come back and *take you to be with me* that you also may be where I am." (NIV)
  「わたしの父の家には住む所がたくさんあります。そうでなかったら、あなたがたのために場所を用意しに行く、と言ったでしょうか。わたしが行って、あなたがたに場所を用意したら、また来て、あなたがたをわたしのもとに迎えます。わたしがいるところに、あなたがたもいるようにするためです。」
  (新改訳 2017)

5. Read Matthew 6:19-21 and 1 Peter 1:3-4. There are rewards kept in heaven for us when we honor God during our life. How are these rewards different from worldly wealth and possessions?

マタイの福音書 6 章 19〜21 節とペテロの手紙第一 1 章 3〜4 節を読みましょう。私達がこの人生において神を敬うと、天に報いが用意されます。これらの報いは世俗的な富や所有物とどのように違いますか？

- Matthew 6:19-21 (マタイの福音書 6 章 19〜21 節)
  "Do not store up for yourselves treasures on earth, where moths and vermin destroy, and where thieves break in and steal. But store up for yourselves *treasures in heaven*, where *moths and vermin do not destroy*, and where *thieves do not break in and steal*. For where your treasure is, there your heart will be also." (NIV)
  「自分のために、地上に宝を蓄えるのはやめなさい。そこでは虫やさびで傷物になり、盗人が壁に穴を開けて盗みます。自分のために、天に宝を蓄えなさい。そこでは虫やさびで傷物になることはなく、盗人が壁に穴を開けて盗むこともありません。あなたの宝のあるところ、そこにあなたの心もあるのです。」(新改訳 2017)

- 1 Peter 1:3-4 (ペテロの手紙第一 1 章 3〜4 節)
  "Praise be to the God and Father of our Lord Jesus Christ! In his great mercy he has given us new birth into a living hope through the resurrection of Jesus Christ from the dead, and into an *inheritance that can never perish, spoil or fade*. This inheritance is *kept in heaven for you*." (NIV)
  「私たちの主イエス・キリストの父である神がほめたたえられますように。神は、ご自分の大きなあわれみのゆえに、イエス・キリストが死者の中からよみがえられたことによって、私たちを新しく生まれさせ・生ける望みを持たせてくださいました。また、朽ちることも、汚れることも、消えて行くこともない資産を受け継ぐようにしてくださいました。これらは、あなたがたのために天に蓄えられています。」(新改訳 2017)

<u>REFLECT</u> (考えましょう)

1. What do you think will happen to you after you die?
   あなた自身が死んだ後、あなたはどうなると思いますか？

2. What happens after you die, according to the Bible?
   聖書によると、人が死んだ後どうなりますか？

3. God offers salvation and eternal life to us through Jesus Christ. Is it hard to receive these generous gifts from Him?
   神はイエス・キリストを通して救いと永遠のいのちを私たちに与えてくださいます。神からこれらの寛大な贈り物を受け取るのは難しいですか？

4. When we know that we will live forever with God, we live life differently on earth now. Someone who believes they will be with God forever in heaven will live their life now to serve Him and thank Him for salvation, rather than living for their own gain. What does it look like to serve God in our daily lives?
   私たちが神と共に永遠に生きることを知ったとき、私たちは地上で違った人生を送ることでしょう。天国で永遠に神と共にいることになると信じる人は、自分の利益のために生きるのではなく、神に仕え、救いに感謝して人生を生きるでしょう。私たちの日常生活の中で、神に仕えるとはどういうことですか？

5. If you believe in eternal life in heaven and salvation through Jesus, how can you help share these gifts with others, who do not yet know about Him?
もしあなたが天国での永遠の命とイエスからの救いを信じるなら、どうやってこれらの贈り物をイエスについてまだ知らない人たちと分かち合うことができますか？

6. Who are some of the people you know who do not yet know about Jesus and the salvation and eternal life that He offers?
あなたの周りで、イエスのこと、また彼が与えてくださる救いと永遠の命についてまだ知らない人は誰ですか？

REVIEW (まとめ)

When we die, we face judgment before the Lord. Jesus offers deliverance from death and the promise of eternal life. Eternal life in heaven is peaceful and beautiful. People who do not believe in Jesus are not yet free from eternal punishment. We can pray for people who do not know Jesus and share the story about Him so that others can receive salvation too.

私たちが死ぬとき、私たちは主の御前で裁きに直面します。イエスは死からの解放と永遠の命の約束を与えてくださっています。天国での永遠の命は平和で美しいものです。イエスを信じていない人々は、まだ永遠の罰から解放されていません。私たちは、イエスを知らない人々のために祈り、イエスについての話を共有することにより、他の人々をも救いに導くことができます。

DISCUSS (話し合いましょう)

1. Do you have any questions about the reading or homework?
   読んだ箇所や宿題について何か質問がありますか？

2. What do you think will happen to you after you die?
   死んだ後に、あなたはどうなると思いますか？

3. According to the Bible, what will happen to people after death?
   聖書によると、死後の人々に何が起こりますか？

4. Do you have any questions about heaven or eternal life?
   あなたは、天国や永遠の命のことについて何か質問がありますか？

5. What can you do for the people in your life who have not accepted Jesus as their Savior and do not know about the gift of eternal life?
   イエスを救い主として受け入れておらず、永遠の命の贈り物について知らない人々にあなたは何ができるでしょうか？

6. Pray as a group for unsaved friends or family members. Pray for any members of the group who would like to believe, but do not yet believe.
   まだ救いを受けていない友人や家族について祈りましょう。信じたいという気持ちがあるのにも関わらず、まだ信じきれていない人々のために祈りましょう。

LIVE IT OUT (活かしましょう)

This week, pray for your friends and family members who do not know Jesus. If you believe that Jesus came to offer salvation from death and the gift of eternal life, then you know how important it is for other people to know Him too. Think about how you could share this hope and future with them. Pray for them, invite them to church, and think of ways to tell them about salvation.

今週、イエスを知らない友人や家族のために祈ってみてください。イエスが死からの救いと永遠のいのちの贈り物を差し出すために来られたと信じるなら、他の人も彼を知ることがどれほど重要なことか分かるでしょう。この希望と未来を人々と分かち合う方法を考えてみてください。彼らのために祈り、教会に招待し、救いについて伝える方法を考えてみましょう。

NOTES (ノート)

WEEK 6
第 6 週

FAITH
信仰

WEEK 6
第 6 週

FAITH
信仰

"...faith comes from hearing the message, and the message
is heard through the word about Christ."
Romans 10:17 (NIV)

「...信仰は聞くことから始まります。聞くことは、
キリストについてのことばを通して実現するのです。」
ローマ人への手紙 10 章 17 節 (新改訳 2017)

FAITH
信仰

Faith is believing and trusting in what we do not see. It is both a choice and a condition of the heart. Having faith in God means believing that He is who He says He is, and that what He says is true. A good example of this in the Bible is the story of Noah.

Noah demonstrated great faith in Genesis 6:9 - Genesis 8:22. God told him to build an ark, because there would be a great flood. Noah believed God, even though those around him did not. He acted in accordance with his belief by building a boat. Then the great flood came, and Noah and his family were safe.

God gives truth and guidance to us today, during our prayer time and through the Bible. When we believe that the Bible is true and that God is good, we apply what we learn from Him to our lives. We act in accordance with our beliefs. We demonstrate faith in God by obeying Him and following His commands.

信仰とは、私たちが見えないものを信じ、信頼することです。信仰とは選択することであり、また心の状態を表しています。神への信仰を持つということは、神がご自分が誰であるか、言っている事をそのまま信じることです。この良い例として挙げられるのが聖書のノアの物語です。

ノアは創世記 6 章 9 節〜8 章 22 節で大きな信仰を示しました。大洪水が起こるので、神は彼に箱舟を造るように言われました。周囲の人々が信じなかったのに、ノアは神を信じました。彼は自分の信念に従って、舟を造ることを行動に移しました。その後大洪水が起こり、ノアと彼の家族は無事でした。

神は今日において、祈りの時間と聖書を通して、真実と導きを与えてくださいます。聖書が真実であり、神が良い方であると信じるとき、私たちは神から学んだことを人生に活かします。私たちは信念に従って行動します。私たちは神に従い、神の命令に従うことによって信仰を示します。

STUDY (学びましょう)

1. What do the following verses tell us about faith?
   次の聖句は信仰について何を教えていますか？

   - Hebrews 11:1 (ヘブル人への手紙 11 章 1 節)
     "Now faith is the *assurance of things hoped for*, the *conviction of things not seen*."
     (ESV)
     「さて、信仰は、望んでいることを保証し、目に見えないものを確信させる
     ものです。」(新改訳 2017)

   - Romans 10:17 (ローマ人への手紙 10 章 17 節)
     "So *faith comes from hearing*, and hearing *through the word of Christ*." (ESV)
     「…信仰は聞くことから始まります。聞くことは、キリストについてのこと
     ばを通して実現するのです。」(新改訳 2017)

   - Hebrews 11:6 (ヘブル人への手紙 11 章 6 節)
     "And *without faith it is impossible to please God*, because anyone who comes to him
     must believe that he exists and that he rewards those who earnestly seek him." (NIV)
     「信仰がなければ、神に喜ばれることはできません。神に近づく者は、神が
     おられることと、神がご自分を求める者には報いてくださる方であることを、
     信じなければならないのです。」(新改訳 2017)

   - 2 Corinthians 5:7 (コリント人への手紙第二 5 章 7 節)
     "For we *walk by faith, not by sight*." (ESV)
     「私たちは見えるものによらず、信仰によって歩んでいます。」
     (新改訳 2017)

2. Read the examples of faith in Hebrews 11:1-31. People who believe God obey Him. Who was the man mentioned in Hebrews 11:7?
   ヘブル人への手紙第 11 章 1〜31 節の信仰の例を読みましょう。神を信じる人々は神に従います。ヘブル人への手紙第 11 章 7 節で書かれている人はだれですか？

3. Read the story of Noah in Genesis 6:9 – Genesis 8:22.
   創世記 6 章 9 節〜 創世記 8 章 22 節のノアの物語を読みましょう。

   a. What did God tell Noah to do in this story? (Genesis 6:13-21)
      この物語の中で、神はノアに何をするように命じましたか？
      (創世記 6 章 13〜21 節)

   b. What did Noah do, in response to the guidance God gave him? (Genesis 6:22)
      神がノアに与えた導きに応えるために、ノアは何をしましたか？
      (創世記 6 章 22 節)

   c. Did Noah demonstrate faith through his actions?
      ノアは自分の行動を通じて信仰を示しましたか？

   d. What happened to the people who did not believe God? (Genesis 7:23)
      神を信じなかった人たちに何が起こりましたか？ （創世記 7 章 23 節）

4. Faith is shown through obedience. When we believe, we follow. What does James 2:22 tell us about the connection between faith and actions?
信仰は従順を通じて現されます。信じるとき、私たちは従います。ヤコブの手紙 2 章 22 節は、信仰と行動の関係について何を教えていますか？

 "You see that his faith and his actions were working together, and his faith was made complete by what he did." (NIV)
「あなたが見ている通り、信仰がその行いとともに働き、信仰は行いによって完成されました。」(新改訳 2017)

REFLECT (考えましょう)

1. God told Noah that there would be a flood. He told him to build a large boat. He listened and obeyed, because he believed God.
神はノアに、洪水が起こることを伝えました。神は彼に大きな舟を造るように言いました。ノアは神を信じていたので神の声に聞き従いました。

    * If God told you to build a boat and move into it, because a flood was coming, would you do it?
洪水が来るから舟を造ってその中に入るようにと、神があなたに伝えたら、あなたはそれに従いますか？

    * Noah's neighbors did not believe in God. They probably thought Noah was crazy when they saw him building his boat. How do you think that made him feel?
ノアの隣人は神を信じませんでした。彼らはノアが舟を造っているのを見て、ノアが狂っていると思ったことでしょう。あなたはそれに対してノアはどんな気持ちになったと思いますか？

2. Sometimes God tells us to do things that do not make sense to other people. Why is it important to follow God, in faith, even if others do not believe what He is telling you?
時々、他の人々には理解し難いことをするように神は私たちに命じます。たとえ他の人が神があなたに言っていることを信じなくても、信仰をもって神に従うことがなぜ重要なのでしょうか？

3. God still speaks to people today. He speaks to us through our prayer time with Him and through the Bible. The Bible is His written word.
今日においても神は人々に語りかけています。神は私達の祈りの時間を通して、そして聖書を通して私達に語りかけます。聖書は神の言葉が書かれた書物です。

- Have you tried applying any of the wisdom and guidance of the Bible to your life?
あなたは自分の人生に聖書の中の知恵と導きを活かそうとしたことはありますか？

- What do you know about prayer?
あなたは祈りについて何を知っていますか？

<u>REVIEW</u> (まとめ)

Having faith is choosing to believe in what God says and act on it. Noah obeyed God because he believed Him. We can declare with our mouths that we believe in God, we can believe with our hearts, and we can demonstrate belief in our actions. Believing is a choice to trust in God.

信仰を持つということは、神が言われることを信じ、それに基づいて行動することを選ぶということです。ノアは神を信じたので、神に従いました。私たちは自分の口で神を信じると宣言し、心から信じ、そして自分の行動により信念を示すことができます。信じることは神を信頼するという選択です。

<u>DISCUSS</u> (話し合いましょう)

1. Do you have any questions about the reading or homework?
   読んだ箇所や宿題について何か質問がありますか？

2. What is faith?
   信仰とは、何ですか？

3. What does it mean to believe?
   信じるとはどういう意味ですか？

4. What did you learn about faith from the story of Noah?
   ノアの物語から信仰について何を学びましたか？

5. If God told you to build a boat and move into it, because a flood was coming, would you do it?
   もし神があなたに洪水が来るので、舟を造ってそこに入るようにと命じられたら、あなたはそれに従いますか？

6. Believing in God means trusting Him. We can choose to trust someone, even if we are not sure what will happen. We can show God our trust and belief in Him by obeying His commands. How can you apply His teaching to your life this week?
   神を信じることとは、神自身を信頼することです。何が起こるのかわからない場合でも、私たちは誰かを信頼するということを選択できます。私たちは神の命令に従うことによって神への信頼と信仰を示すことができます。今週どのようにあなたは神の教えを自分の人生に活かせますか？

<u>LIVE IT OUT</u> (活かしましょう)

Apply some of the principles from the Bible to your life this week. Choose to believe that what God said is true and obey it. You will not be disappointed. God is faithful and He will show you the truth in His words. Remember, we walk in faith because He first loved us, not to earn His love. We trust in God, because He is good and loving.

If you would like to believe in God, but you are still having trouble believing, pray and ask God to help you overcome your unbelief. Also pray for the other members of this group who would like to grow in their faith.

今週、聖書の御言葉をご自分の生活に当てはめてみましょう。神が言ったことは真実であると信じ、それに従ってみましょう。それによって失望することはありません。神は忠実なお方で、神はみ言葉で真実を示します。思い出してください。神が最初に私たちを愛してくださったからこそ、私たちは信仰に歩めるのです。神の愛を得るためではありません。私たちが神を信頼するのは神が善良で愛にあふれているからです。

神を信じたいと思っているのに、まだ信じることが難しいのであれば、祈り、不信仰に打ち勝てるよう神に助けを求めてください。 信仰のうちに成長したいと願っている他のメンバーのためにも祈りましょう。

Reference verses: Romans 10:11; Luke 11:28; Proverbs 3:5-6; Psalm 37:5-6
参照聖句：ローマ人への手紙 10 章 11 節; ルカの福音書 11 章 28 節; 箴言 3 章 5〜6 節; 詩篇 37 篇 5〜6 節

<u>NOTES</u> (ノート)

NOTES (ノート)

WEEK 6

WEEK 7
第 7 週

GRACE
恵み

WEEK 7
第 7 週

GRACE
恵み

"For by grace you have been saved through faith. And this is not your own doing;
it is the gift of God, not a result of works, so that no one may boast."
Ephesians 2:8-9 (ESV)

「この恵みのゆえに、あなたがたは信仰によって救われたのです。
それはあなたがたから出たことではなく、神の賜物です。
行いによるのではありません。だれも誇ることのないためです。」
エペソ人への手紙 2 章 8〜9 節 (新改訳 2017)

GRACE
恵み

Grace is showing favor to someone who does not deserve it, simply because you care about that person. Parents show grace to children. Parents want children to behave and obey them, but they also know that children cannot act like adults, because they are not adults. They do not have the maturity to be able to obey their parents well all the time. Parents are proud of them when they obey, and they try to be patient with them and extend grace when they disobey.

In the same way, God has grace with us. He wants us to obey Him, but He is patient with us, extends grace and forgives when we disobey. We should try our best to obey God, but we can be at peace knowing that even when we make mistakes, He still loves us. When we repent, He forgives us. He shows grace to those who trust and believe in Him, because of the sacrifice of Jesus.

恵みとは、好意を受けるには価しない人に好意を示すことです。あなたがその人のことを大切に思っているという単純な理由で、恵みを与えます。親は子供たちに恵みを与えます。両親は子供たちに行儀よく、従順になってくれることを願っていますが、同時に、子供は大人ではないので、大人のように振る舞うことができないことも知っています。子供たちは両親に常に従うことができるほどまだ成熟していません。両親は子供が自分のいうことをきいてくれたとき、誇りに思います。子供に対して忍耐強くなれるように努力し、また子供が従わないときには忍耐強く待ち、恵みを与えます。

同じように、神は私たちに恵みを与えてくださいます。神は私たちが神に従うことを望んでいますが、辛抱強く私たちを見守り、さらなる恵みを与え、私たちが不従順に歩むときでさえ赦しを与えてくださいます。私たちは神に従うように最善を尽くすべきですが、私たちがたとえ間違えを犯しても、神は私たちを愛してくださっており、私たちはその愛を知ることで平安を得ることができます。私たちが悔い改めると、神は赦しを与えてくださいます。イエスが犠牲になったため、神はご自身を信じ、信頼する人たちに対して、恵みを示してくださいます。

__STUDY__ (学びましょう)

1. Read Luke 15:11-31. This is a story Jesus told that demonstrates grace.
   ルカの福音書 15 章 11〜31 節を読みましょう。ここでイエスは恵が示されること
   を例え話を用いて話されました。

   a. What did the younger son do that was wrong? (Luke 15:12-13)
      弟がしたことで何が間違っていましたか？（ルカの福音書 15 章 12〜13 節）

   b. The son realized he did wrong and repented. Instead of punishing him, the father
      forgave him and showed him grace. What did the father do in Luke 15:20-24?
      息子は自分が間違いを犯したことを悟り、悔い改めました。父親は彼を罰す
      る代わりに、彼を赦し、彼に恵みを示しました。父親はルカの福音書 15 章 20
      〜24 節で何をしましたか？

2. Read Luke 22:1 – Luke 23:43. Jesus was betrayed, mocked, beaten, and crucified. He
   suffered a painful death, so that He could defeat death. He took our punishment for sin,
   so that we could be set free. His sacrifice was the ultimate act of grace.
   ルカの福音書 22 章 1 節〜23 章 43 節を読みましょう。イエスは裏切られ、嘲笑
   され、殴られ、十字架にかけられました。彼は苦痛な死を経験しそれによって死
   を打ち負かしました。私たちを罪から解放するために、イエスは私たちの罪の罰
   を代わりに受けました。彼の犠牲は究極の恵みでした。

   a. What are some of the bad things that people said and did to Jesus, in this passage?
      この聖書の箇所で、人々がイエスに対して言ったり、行ったりした悪いこと
      は何でしたか？

   b. How did He respond to them? (Luke 23:34)
      イエスはどのように彼らに応えましたか？（ルカの福音書 23 章 34 節）

3. Jesus forgave those who hurt Him. They deserved punishment, but even while He was on the cross, He showed them grace. What does this response teach you about grace and the love of Jesus?

イエスは自分を傷つけた人々をお赦しになられました。傷つけた人々は罰を受けるに価しますが、イエスは十字架につけられていた間でさえ、そんな彼らに恵みを与えました。この行動は、恵みとイエスの愛についてあなたに何を教えていますか？

4. What do the following verses teach us about the grace of God?

次の聖句は神の恵みについて私たちに何を教えていますか？

- Ephesians 2:8-9 (エペソ人への手紙 2 章 8〜9 節)
"For *by grace you have been saved* through faith. And this is not your own doing; it is the gift of God, not a result of works, so that no one may boast." (ESV)
「この恵みのゆえに、あなたがたは信仰によって救われたのです。それはあなたがたから出たことではなく、神の賜物です。行いによるのではありません。だれも誇ることのないためです。」(新改訳 2017)

- Titus 3:7 (テトスへの手紙 3 章 7 節)
"…so that being *justified by his grace* we might *become heirs* according to the hope of eternal life." (ESV)
「それは、私たちがキリストの恵みによって義と認められ、永遠のいのちの望みを抱く相続人となるためでした。」(新改訳 2017)

- Romans 6:14 (ローマ人への手紙 6 章 14 節)
"For *sin shall no longer be your master*, because you are *not under the law, but under grace.*" (NIV)
「罪があなたがたを支配することはないからです。あなたがたは律法の下にではなく、恵みの下にあるのです。」(新改訳 2017)

5. What does Romans 3:20-24 teach about trying to earn God's favor?
    ローマ人への手紙 3 章 20〜24 節は、神の好意を勝ち取ろうとすることについて
    何を教えていますか?

"Therefore no one will be declared righteous in God's sight by the works of the law; rather, through the law we become conscious of our sin. But now apart from the law the righteousness of God has been made known, to which the Law and the Prophets testify. This righteousness is given through faith in Jesus Christ to all who believe. There is no difference between Jew and Gentile, for all have sinned and fall short of the glory of God, and all are justified freely by his grace through the redemption that came by Christ Jesus." (NIV)

「なぜなら、人はだれも、律法を行うことによっては神の前に義と認められない
からです。律法を通して生じるのは罪の意識です。しかし今や、律法とは関わり
なく、律法と預言者たちの書によって証しされて、神の義が示されました。すな
わち、イエス・キリストを信じることによって、信じるすべての人に与えられる
神の義です。そこに差別はありません。すべての人は罪を犯して、神の栄光を受
けることができず、神の恵みにより、キリスト・イエスによる贖いを通して、価
なしに義と認められるからです。」(新改訳 2017)

REFLECT (考えましょう)

1. Can you think of a time when you have seen someone show forgiveness or grace to someone who did not deserve it?
誰かが、恵みを受けるに価しない人に対して赦しや恵みを示すのを見たことがありますか？

2. The truth is that none of us deserve forgiveness or grace. We are sinners, and our sin creates a barrier between us and the most Holy God. We cannot erase sin by doing good things. Do you ever try to earn God's favor?
真実は、私たちの中で誰も赦しや恵みに価しないということです。私たちは罪人であり、私たちの罪は最も聖なる神との間に障壁を作ります。良いことをしても罪を消すことはできません。今まで神の好意を勝ち取ろうとしたことはありますか？

3. God's grace is a gift that He offers freely to those who repent and believe in Him. Is it hard for you to accept God's gift of grace?
神の恵みは、悔い改め、神を信じる人々に捧げられる無償の贈り物です。神の恵みの賜物を受け入れることはあなたにとって難しいですか？

4. The grace of God changes the reason why we serve. We no longer serve Him to earn His favor. We serve Him, in gratitude, because of His favor. Does knowing how much God loves you make you want to serve Him?
神の恵みは、私たちが仕える理由を変えます。私たちはもはや彼の好意を得る目的のために仕えません。私たちが感謝を持って仕える理由は神が私たちにしてくださった好意のゆえです。神があなたをどれほど愛しているかを知ったことで、あなたは神に仕えたいと思うようになりますか？

REVIEW (まとめ)

Grace is unmerited favor. God looked past our wrongs and offered forgiveness, simply because He cares for us. We have not earned it and we do not deserve it. He did this because He wants to have a relationship with us. We are saved by grace alone, through faith, and not by works.

恵みは私たちには受けるに相応しくない恩恵です。神は私たちが犯した過ちを見逃して、神が私たちを愛してくださっているからという単純な理由で赦しを与えてくださるのです。私たちはその赦しを勝ち取った訳でも、またそれに価する訳でもありません。神が私たちと関係を持ちたい、関わりたいと思っているからこその恵みです。私たちは、信仰を通し、恵みによってのみ救われるのであり、自分の働きによって救われるわけではないのです。

DISCUSS (話し合いましょう)

1. Do you have any questions about the reading or homework?
   読んだ箇所や宿題について何か質問がありますか？

2. What is grace?
   恵みとは何ですか？

3. Can you think of an example of someone showing grace?
   誰かが恵みを見せてくれた例を考えることができますか？

4. Do you ever feel pressure to earn favor from people?
   あなたは今まで人々から好意を得るためにプレッシャーを感じることがありますか？

5. Does it feel freeing to know that you do not have to earn God's favor?
   自分の力で神の好意を勝ち取る必要はないと知って、安堵しますか？

6. God gave us grace, forgiveness, love, and salvation through Jesus. Do you appreciate and want this from Him?
   神はイエスを通して、私たちに恵み、赦し、愛、そして救いを与えてくださいました。神から与えられるものを感謝し、また受け取りたいと思いますか？

7. Does knowing about God's generosity and grace make you want to know Him more?
   神の寛大さと恵みについて理解することで、あなたはもっと神を知りたいと思いますか？

LIVE IT OUT (活かしましょう)

Think of someone who has done wrong to you. Show them grace this week. Forgive them and let go of any bitterness toward them. Pray for them, encourage them, bless them, and serve them. Show them love and respect. Do something to make them feel special and show them they are valuable. Ask God to help you. It is hard to show grace to people who do not deserve it, but we can do it with the strength that the Lord provides.

あなたにあやまちを犯した人のことを考えてみてください。今週その人たちに恵みを示してください。彼らを赦し、彼らへ否定的な思いを手放してください。彼らのために祈り、励まし、祝福し、仕えてください。彼らに愛と尊敬を示しましょう。その人たちが特別な存在であると感じるような、また彼らが貴重な存在であることを示すようなことを何かをしてみてください。神に助けを求めてください。それに価しない人々に恵みを示すのは難しいことですが、主が与えてくださる力でそれをすることができます。

NOTES (ノート)

NOTES (ノート)

WEEK 8
第8週

WALKING WITH GOD
神と共に歩む

WEEK 8
第8週

WALKING WITH GOD
神と共に歩む

"Jesus replied, "Anyone who loves me will *obey my teaching.*
My Father will love them, and *we will come to them and make our home with them.*"
John 14:23 (NIV)

「イエスは彼に答えられた。「だれでもわたしを愛する人は、
わたしのことばを守ります。そうすれば、わたしの父はその人を愛し、
わたしたちはその人のところに来て、その人とともに住みます。」
ヨハネの福音書 14 章 23 節 (新改訳 2017)

WALKING WITH GOD
神と共に歩む

When we decide to follow Jesus, we become a part of His family. We spend time with Him, talk with Him through prayer, and serve Him, as we would do for our parents or other family members. We spend time with Him by praying, reading our Bible, and living in fellowship with the community of believers, which is the body of Christ. We serve Him by loving Him, loving others, and obeying His commands. We learn from the Bible how to honor Him in all that we do.

Start building a habit of seeking Him and walking with Him daily. It is helpful to have specific time set aside in the day to pray and read your Bible, even if it is only 5-10 minutes. Pick a time and place with fewer distractions, so that you can focus on listening to the Lord and learning from Him. It is also good to start practicing praying continually. As you go throughout the day, think of ways to include, seek, and honor God in it. Pray for the people you interact with and seek the Lord's guidance in your activities. Find and stay connected with a local church that helps you learn to live in fellowship with Him.

イエスに従うことを決めたとき、私たちは神の家族の一員になります。私たちは、両親や他の家族と時間を過ごすのと同じように、神と時間を過ごし、祈りを通して神と話し、神に仕えます。 私たちは祈り、聖書を読んで、キリストの身体である信者のコミュニティの交わりの中で生きることによって、神と時間を過ごします。神を愛し、他の人を愛し、神の命令に従うことによって、私たちは神に仕えます。私たちは聖書から、私たちが行うすべてのことにおいて神を敬う方法を学びます。

毎日、神を求め、神と一緒に歩む習慣を身につけましょう。たとえ5〜10分でも、1日の中で決まった時間を確保して祈り、聖書を読みます。主に耳を傾け、主から学ぶことに集中できるように、気を散らさない時間と場所を選びましょう。また、絶えず祈りの練習を始めるのも良いことです。あなたが一日を通して、神と共に過ごし、神を求め、そして尊敬する方法を考えて見ましょう。一緒に時間を過ごす人々のために祈り、主の導きがあなたの活動の中にあるよう求めてください。あなたが神と共に過ごす人生について学ぶことができる地元の教会を見つけて、その教会につながりましょう。

__STUDY__ (学びましょう)

1. What do the following verses show us about having a relationship with God?
   次の聖句は、神と交わりを持つことについて私たちに何を示していますか？

   - Matthew 22:37-39 (マタイの福音書 22 章 37〜39 節)
     "Jesus replied: *'Love the Lord your God with all your heart and with all your soul and with all your mind.'* This is the first and greatest commandment. And the second is like it: *'Love your neighbor as yourself.'*" (NIV)
     「イエスは彼に言われた。「『あなたは心を尽くし、いのちを尽くし、知性を尽くして、あなたの神、主を愛しなさい。』これが、重要な第一の戒めです。『あなたの隣人を自分自身のように愛しなさい。』という第二の戒めも、それと同じように重要です。」(新改訳 2017)

   - John 15:15 (ヨハネの福音書 15 章 15 節)
     "No longer do I call you servants, for the servant does not know what his master is doing; but I have called you *friends*, for all that I have heard from my Father I have made known to you." (ESV)
     「わたしはもう、あなたがたをしもべとは呼びません。しもべなら主人が何をするのか知らないからです。わたしはあなたがたを友と呼びました。父から聞いたことをすべて、あなたがたには知らせたからです。」(新改訳 2017)

   - John 14:23 (ヨハネの福音書 14 章 23 節)
     "Jesus replied, "Anyone who loves me will *obey my teaching*. My Father will love them, and *we will come to them and make our home with them*." (NIV)
     「イエスは彼に答えられた。「だれでもわたしを愛する人は、わたしのことばを守ります。そうすれば、わたしの父はその人を愛し、わたしたちはその人のところに来て、その人とともに住みます。」(新改訳 2017)

- 1 Chronicles 16:11 (歴代誌第一 16 章 11 節)
  "Seek the Lord and his strength; seek his presence continually!" (ESV)
  「主とその御力を尋ね求めよ。絶えず御顔を慕い求めよ。」(新改訳 2017)

- James 5:13 (ヤコブの手紙 5 章 13 節)
  "Is anyone among you suffering? Let him pray. Is anyone cheerful? Let him sing praise." (ESV)
  「あなたがたの中に苦しんでいる人がいれば、その人は祈りなさい。喜んでいる人がいれば、その人は賛美しなさい。」(新改訳 2017)

2. What do the following verses teach us about prayer?
   次の聖句は、祈りについて何を教えていますか？

   - 1 Thessalonians 5:16-18 (テサロニケ人への手紙第一 5 章 16〜18 節)
     "Rejoice always, pray without ceasing, give thanks in all circumstances; for this is the will of God in Christ Jesus for you." (ESV)
     「いつも喜んでいなさい。絶えず祈りなさい。すべてのことにおいて感謝しなさい。これが、イエス・キリストにあって神があなたがたに望んでおられることです。」(新改訳 2017)

   - Matthew 7:7 (マタイの福音書 7 章 7 節)
     "Ask and it will be given to you; seek and you will find; knock and the door will be opened to you." (NIV)
     「求めなさい。そうすれば与えられます。探しなさい。そうすれば見出します。たたきなさい。そうすれば開かれます。」(新改訳 2017)

3. What do the following verses teach about Scripture?
    次の聖句は、聖書のことについて何を教えていますか？

    *   2 Timothy 3:16 (テモテへの手紙第二 3 章 16 節)
        "All Scripture is *God-breathed* and is *useful for teaching, rebuking, correcting and training in righteousness...*" (NIV)
        「聖書はすべて神の霊感によるもので、教えと戒めと矯正と義の訓練のために有益です。」(新改訳 2017)

    *   Psalm 119:105 (詩篇 119 篇 105 節)
        "Your word is a lamp to my feet and a *light to my path.*" (ESV)
        「あなたのみことばは　私の足のともしび　私の道の光です。」
        (新改訳 2017)

    *   Proverbs 3:1-2 (箴言 3 章 1〜2 節)
        "My son, do not forget my teaching, but keep my commands in your heart, for they will *prolong your life many years* and *bring you peace and prosperity.*" (NIV)
        「わが子よ、私の教えを忘れるな。心に私の命令を保つようにせよ。長い日々と、いのちと平安の年月が、あなたに増し加えられるからだ。」
        (新改訳 2017)

4. Psalm 119:9-16 is a declaration of commitment to seek and follow the Lord, from a man who truly loves the Lord. What can we learn from this passage about walking with God?
    詩篇 119 篇 9〜16 節は、主を真に愛する人が、主を求めて従うことを約束する宣言です。私たちが神と共に歩むことについてこの箇所から何が学べるでしょうか？

5. What does Joshua 1:8 teach about studying Scripture?
   ヨシュア記 1 章 8 節は、聖書を学ぶことについて何を教えていますか？

   "Keep this Book of the Law always on your lips; *meditate on it day and night*, so that you may be careful to *do everything written in it*. Then you will be prosperous and successful." (NIV)
   「このみおしえの書をあなたの口から離さず、昼も夜もそれを口ずさめ。そのうちに記されていることすべてを守り行うためである。そのとき、あなたは自分がすることで繁栄し、そのとき、あなたは栄えるからである。」(新改訳 2017)

<u>REFLECT</u> (考えましょう)

1. What does "loving others" look like?
   他人を愛するとは、具体的にはどういうことですか？

2. What does it mean to love God? (John 14:15)
   神を愛するとは、どういう意味ですか？ （ヨハネの福音書 14 章 15 節）

3. Read Revelation 3:20. Jesus is waiting to have a relationship with us. Would you like to have a deeper relationship with Him?
   ヨハネの黙示録 3 章 20 節を読みましょう。イエスは私たちとの交わりを持つために待ち望んでいます。あなたはイエスともっと深い交わりを持ちたいですか？

REVIEW (まとめ)

God wants to have a relationship with you. We can have a relationship with Him by praying, reading our Bibles, and worshipping Him. People who love God serve, obey, and honor Him.

神はあなたとの交わりを求めています。私たちは、祈って聖書を読み、そして神を崇拝することによって神との交わりを持つことができます。神を愛する人々は神に仕え、従い、そして栄光をたたえます。

DISCUSS (話し合いましょう)

1. Do you have any questions about the reading or homework?
   読んだ箇所や宿題について何か質問がありますか？

2. What do you think it means to have a relationship with God? If you are not sure, think about how you would invest in a relationship with a friend or family member.
   あなたは、神との交わりを持つことが何を意味していると思いますか？ よくわからない場合は、友人や家族との関係を深めるため、自分が何をするかを考えてみてください。

3. Communication is an important part of a relationship. Prayer is a time of listening and talking with God. How can you pray to God?
   コミュニケーションは関係を強くするために大事なことです。祈りは神に耳を傾け、神と話す時間です。あなたはどうやって神に祈ることができますか？

4. Why should we pray?
   なぜ私たちは祈る必要があるのですか？

5. Reading the Bible is another important part of spending time with God. Why do you think reading the Bible is important?
   聖書を読むことは、神と過ごす時間の中で、もう一つの重要な部分です。なぜ聖書を読むことが重要だと思いますか？

6. Do you have any questions about how to have a relationship with God?
   神との交わりを持つことについて、何か質問がありますか？

7. How can you deepen your relationship with God this week?
   今週どうやって神との関係を深めることができますか？

LIVE IT OUT (活かしましょう)

Think of one thing in your relationship with God that you would like to improve. What can you do differently this week to grow closer to Him? Some examples of things that you can focus on are praying, worshipping, reading your Bible, serving, and obeying God. Select and focus on one of these. Ask God to help you grow in your relationship with Him.

神との交わりの中で、改善したいと思うことを一つ考えてください。今週神にさらに近づき成長するために、何かこれまでと違うことができますか？焦点を当てることのいくつかの例は、祈り、礼拝、聖書を読むこと、神に仕えること、従うことです。これらのことのどれかにおいて、１つ選んでそれに集中してみましょう。神との交わりを持つ中であなたの成長のために神が助けて下さるよう求めましょう。

FINAL INSTRUCTIONS (最後に)

Review "The Gospel Message" in the next section. Students can use the illustrations to explain Christianity and share the good news with their friends and family members. This might also be a good time to review the "Christian Vocabulary List," answer any questions the group has from this book and discuss the plan for the next Bible study.

グループとして、次のセクションの「福音のメッセージ」を復習しましょう。生徒の皆さんは、キリスト教について説明し、良い知らせを友人や家族と共有するためにイラストを使用してもいいです。「クリスチャン語彙リスト」を復習し、この本でグループから出た質問に答え、次のバイブルスタディの計画について話し合うのにもよい時期かもしれません。

NOTES (ノート)

NOTES (ノート)

The Gospel Message
福音のメッセージ

Now that you have learned the foundational principles of Christianity, let's go back and review the gospel, or the "good news" message about Jesus. This series of illustrations shows the separation from God that exists because of sin. Death is the consequence of sin. No amount of good works can help someone to escape this consequence. Salvation through Jesus is the only way to be reconciled with God. Those who believe in Jesus gain eternal life.

キリスト教の基本原則を学んできましたが、イエスについての福音、または「良い知らせ」のメッセージを振りかえってみてみましょう。下記の一連の図は、罪が原因で起こった神からの分離を示しています。死は罪の結果です。自分は良い行いをしたからといってこの結末から逃れることはできません。イエスを通しての救いこそが、神と和解するための唯一の方法です。イエスを信じる者は永遠の命を得るのです。

PART 1: THE GARDEN OF EDEN
パート 1：エデンの園

In the beginning, God created the world, and He created mankind. Adam and Eve were the first two people He created. They had a close relationship with God, because they had never sinned. God is holy and perfect, and only people without sin can be in His presence.

初めに、神は世界を創造し、人類を創造しました。アダムとイブは、神が創造した最初の 2 人でした。彼らは全く罪を犯したことがなかったので、神と密接な関係を持っていました。神は聖なる方で完全であり、罪のない人々だけが神と一緒にいられます。

PART 2: THE FALL OF MAN
パート 2 ：人の堕落

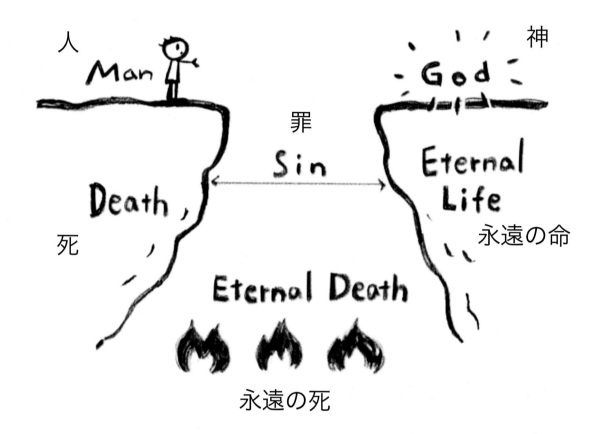

Later, man sinned against God. The relationship between God and man was broken. Sin separated man from God. Sin is not just a severe crime. Any act of disobedience against God is a sin. Some examples of sin are unkindness, impatience, anger, pride, lying, and not forgiving others. Every person has sinned.

The punishment for sin is death. People face a first death in the body. Those who are not saved will face a second, eternal death. Those who remain in a broken relationship with God will be judged and cast into the lake of fire, where there is great pain and suffering.

その後、人は神に対して罪を犯しました。神と人間の関係は壊れていました。罪は人を神から引き離しました。罪は単なる重大な犯罪だけではありません。神に対する不従順な行為は罪です。罪の例には、不親切、焦り、怒り、誇り、嘘、他人を許さないことなどがあります。すべての人が罪を犯しています。

罪に対する罰は死です。人々は最初に起こる肉体の死に直面します。救われていない人々は二度目の死である永遠の死に直面します。神との壊れた関係にとどまる人々は裁かれ、大きな痛みと苦しみに満ちた火の池に投げ込まれます。

PART 3: THE PROBLEM OF MAN
パート 3：人の問題

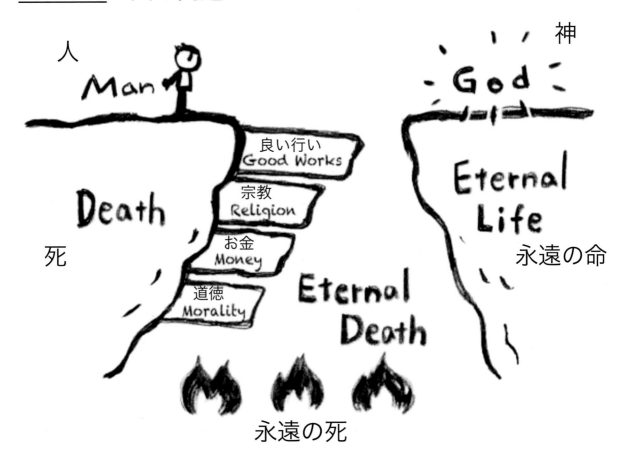

No man can fix his relationship with God by his own effort. No amount of good works can erase sin. No amount of religious behavior, morality, money, or success can save a man from facing judgment and eternal death. On his own, man is destined to spend eternity apart from God.

いかなる努力を持ってでも、誰も神との関係を回復することはできません。善い行いをどんなにしても、罪を消すことはできません。いかなる宗教的な行いや、道徳、金銭または成功も、裁きと永遠の死に直面することから人を救うことはできません。人間は自分の力だけでは、神から離れて永遠に過ごすように定められています。

PART 4: SALVATION
パート 4：救い

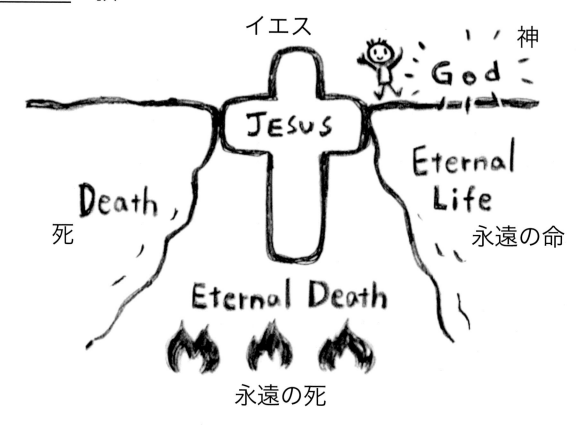

However, God loved the people He created, and chose to save them. He sent His son Jesus down to earth to save us. Jesus is the Son of God, and He Himself is God. He gave His life for us by dying on the cross. He took the penalty of our sins, which He did not deserve, because He had committed no sin. He was perfect and holy.

Then, three days later, He defeated death and rose again. As the risen Savior, Jesus offered salvation to mankind. Whoever believes in Jesus will be saved. Believers can cross from death to life and be reconciled with God. All who repent and believe are forgiven of their sins and will have eternal life with God in heaven.

しかし、神は彼が創造された人々を愛し、私たちを救うことを選びました。神は私たちを救うために息子イエスを地上に遣わされました。イエスは神の子であり、彼自身が神です。イエスは十字架で死ぬことによって、私たちのために命を与えられました。彼は罪を犯さなかったにもかかわらず、私たちの罪の罰を受けました。彼は完全で聖い方でした。

それから、3 日後、彼は死を征服し、よみがえりました。復活した救い主として、イエスは人類に救いを捧げました。イエスを信じる者は救われます。信者は死からいのちへと渡り、神と和解することができます。悔い改め、信じる者は皆、罪を赦され、天国で神と共に永遠のいのちを得ます。

THE GOSPEL MESSAGE

THE NEXT STEP
次のステップ

Do you want to follow Jesus? If so, pray and ask Jesus to be your Savior. Start following and obeying Him. Continue reading your Bible and praying to God. Reading and studying the Bible are important parts of growing in your relationship with God.

Get connected with a local church. This is another important part of your journey. Church is a place where you can connect with other followers of Christ, learn more about the Bible, and encourage and pray for one another. Study Scripture with Bible study groups too. The more time you spend in prayer, in reading the Bible, and in fellowship, the more you will grow.

After you get connected with a church, talk to your pastor or Bible study leader about getting baptized. This is a brief ceremony involving immersion in water and a public declaration of your faith. Baptism symbolizes being washed clean of sin. Your church community will want to support you and celebrate this special decision with you.

Jesus is our hope. With Him, we have joy, peace, and purpose. He gives us love, and He gives us direction. Seek HIm and seek to honor Him in everything that you do. Start walking with Him, and He will change your life.

イエスについて行きたいと思っていますか？もしそう思っているなら、聖書を読み続け、神に祈り続けてください。神と時間を過ごしてください。聖書を読み学ぶことは、神との関係において成長するために重要なことです。

近所にある教会と繋がりを持ってください。教会とつながることは、あなたの信仰の道のりの中で重要な部分となります。教会は、キリストに習う人々とつながり、聖書についてもっと学び、互いに励まし、祈ることができる場所です。バイブルスタディでも聖書を学んでください。祈り、聖書を読むこと、交わりに費やす時間が増えるほど、あなたは成長します。

イエスに従うことを決めたら、洗礼（バプテスマ）を受けることについて牧師に相談してください。洗礼とは、水に浸ることで、罪の洗い流しを象徴する、悔い改めと信仰を公的に宣言する短い儀式です。

イエスは私たちの希望です。彼と共にいることで、私たちには喜び、平和、目的があります。イエスは私たちに愛と導きを与えます。イエスを求め、あなたが行うすべてのことにおいて彼を尊敬する心を求めてください。イエスと歩み始めてください。イエスがあなたの人生を変えるでしょう。

About the Bible
聖書について

For those of you who are new to studying the Bible, you will need to obtain one. I recommend having a hard copy in your own language, and also downloading it onto your phone, or at least knowing how to look up verses online. Make sure you are reading from a good translation too. Not all translations are accurate and reliable.

聖書を勉強するのが初めての人は、まず聖書を手に入れる必要があります。自分の言語で書かれた聖書を手に入れるか、スマートフォンにダウンロードするか、少なくともオンラインで聖句を調べる方法を学ぶことをお勧めします。自分が良い翻訳のバージョンを読んでいることを確認してください。 すべての翻訳が正確で信頼できるとは限らないからです。

FINDING A BIBLE
聖書を見つける

You can find a Bible online, through your church, or at a Christian bookstore. Regular bookstores may also have them. The Bible is translated into many different languages. Bilingual Bibles are also available.

Be careful when choosing a Bible translation. Do not just select the first one you find. Many different people and organizations have translated the books of Bible from their original languages. Some translations are better and more accurate than others. Since most people do not know Hebrew, Aramaic, and Greek, it is important to choose a translation that reflects the meaning of the original text as closely as possible.

教会やキリスト教の書店またはオンラインで聖書を見つけることができます。通常の書店にもあるかもしれません。聖書は多くの異なる言語に翻訳されています。バイリンガルの聖書も出版されています。

気をつけて翻訳を選んでください。最初に見つけた翻訳を単純に選ばないでください。多くのさまざまな人々や組織が最初に書かれた元々の言語から聖書を翻訳しています。一部の翻訳は他の翻訳よりも優れており、より正確です。私たちの多くはヘブライ語、アラム語、ギリシャ語を知らないので、原文の意味にできるだけ反映している翻訳を選択することが重要です。

CHOOSING A TRANSLATION
翻訳の選択

There are two types of translation approaches: word-for-word and thought-for-thought. Word-for-word translations attempt to get the most accurate meaning of the words. While the words may be translated more accurately, the meaning may be harder to understand within the different cultural contexts. The reader will need to ask more questions and do research to understand exactly what is meant by the verses.

Thought-for-thought translations convey the meaning of the phrase or sentence in language that is easier to understand, but they may not be as accurate to the original text. They rely on the understanding of the translator, who may or may not truly understand the depth of the verse. While these translations are more understandable, they should not be consulted as a primary translation, because they may mislead the reader about what the text is actually saying.

A good translation for someone who is new to reading the Bible would be one that is a balance between the two. It should be as accurate as possible, but also understandable. The English versions that we recommend are the 1984 New International Version (NIV), the English Standard Version (ESV) and the New American Standard Bible (NASB). The ESV and NASB are more closely aligned with the original text, but the reader will have to look up more words and context to understand the verses. The Japanese version that we recommend is the 2017 version of the New Japanese Bible (NJB) (Seisho Shinkaiyaku).

翻訳アプローチには、単語ごとに翻訳する方法と、思考や意味を捉えて翻訳する考え方の 2 種類があります。単語ごとの翻訳では、単語の最も正確な意味を翻訳しようという意図があります。単語はより正確に翻訳されるかもしれませんが、異なる文化的文脈の中で意味を理解することは難しいかもしれません。読者はより多くの質問をし、聖句が意味するものを正確に理解するために調べる必要があります。

意味を捉えて行う翻訳は、理解しやすい文章や語句に翻訳されていますが、原文に対して正確ではない場合があります。内容は翻訳者の理解に依存しており、その翻訳者は、聖句の深い意味を本当に理解しているかもしれないし、していないかもしれません。このタイプの翻訳はより理解しやすいものですが、原文の聖書が実際に言っていることについて読者を誤解させる可能性があるため、主要な翻訳として検討すべきではありません。

聖書を読むのが初めての人のための良い翻訳は、2 つのタイプのバランスをとったものでしょう。できる限り正確である必要がありますが、理解可能なものでもなければなりません。推奨される英語版は、新国際版聖書 1984 年版(NIV)、英語標準版聖書（ESV）および新アメリカ標準聖書（NASB）です。ESV と NASB は原典により近く翻訳されていますが、読者は理解するためには言葉や背景を調べたりする必要があります。推奨する日本語版は、2017 年版の新改訳聖書（NJB）です。

LOOKING UP VERSES
聖句の探し方

Once you obtain a Bible, you will have verses and passages to look up in the assigned homework. First, start by finding the book you are looking for in the table of contents. There are 66 books in the Bible. Once you go to the book, the verses are divided into chapters. The chapters and the verses are numbered.

A passage is a section that contains a range of verses. Luke 2:1-21 is an example of a passage. "Luke" is the name of the book. The passage is in Chapter 2. It starts at Verse 1 and ends at Verse 21.

聖書を手に入れたら、宿題の中で聖句を調べることとなります。まず、目次で探している書を見つけることから始めます。聖書には 66 巻の書があります。その書に行くと、聖句は章（詩篇のみ篇）に分かれています。章と節には番号が付けられています。

パッセージは、一連の節を含むセクションです。例えばルカの福音書 2 章 1〜21 節では、「ルカの福音書」は書の名前です。パッセージは 2 章にあります。1 節で始まり、21 節で終わります。

HOW TO STUDY THE BIBLE
聖書の学び方

The books of the Bible were written by many different authors. The various books have different purposes and were written to different audiences, but all contain information that is helpful for us. When you start reading through a book in the Bible, learn a little bit about the context, and it will help you better understand what it is that you are reading. Stop to summarize what you read. Write down the questions you have about it. Think about what it teaches about God and what you can learn from the verse or passage.

聖書の本は多くの異なる著者によって書かれました。それぞれの書には色々な目的があり、また様々な読者に向けて書かれていますが、聖書のすべては私たちにとって役立つ内容です。 聖書の一つの書を読み始めたら、文脈や背景について少し学ぶと、読んでいる部分をより理解することができます。 あなたが読んだ部分の概要をまとめましょう。質問があれば書き留めてください。 聖句が神について何を教えているか、そしてあなたがその聖句から学べることを考えてください。

THE BOOKS OF THE BIBLE
聖書の書

The Bible contains 66 books, divided into the New and Old Testaments. The Old Testament contains the books that were written before Jesus came, and the New Testament contains the books that were written after His death and resurrection. Most of the books in the New Testament were written by leaders of the early church. Most of them knew and walked with Jesus.

The Old Testament contains historical books, books of the Law of God, wisdom literature, and books written by the prophets, who received revelations directly from God. While all of the books are beneficial, some of the best books to start with are Genesis, Exodus, and Proverbs. Genesis and Exodus include history of the world and the Israelites. Many of the stories in those books are referenced in church and in the New Testament. Proverbs is a helpful book of wisdom that can easily be applied to daily life.

The New Testament contains the gospels, early church history, letters written by the early church leaders, and prophetic literature. The gospels, named after their authors Matthew, Mark, Luke, and John, all tell the story of Jesus. This is a good place to start in the New Testament. Acts shows the history of the early church, and Romans through Jude are all letters written to teach and edify the church. Revelation is a prophetic book regarding the end times.

聖書には 66 巻の書があり、新約聖書と旧約聖書に分かれています。旧約聖書にはイエスがこの世に来る前に書かれた本がまとめられており、新約聖書の本はイエスの死と復活の後に書かれたものが収められています。新約聖書のほとんどの本は、初期の教会の指導者たちによって書かれており、その多くの指導者たちは実際にイエスに会い、イエスと共に歩みました。

旧約聖書には、歴史的な書、神の律法の書、知恵の文学、および神から直接啓示を受けた預言者によって書かれた書が含まれています。すべての書は有益ですが、最初に読むのに最適な書は創世記、出エジプト記、箴言です。創世記と出エジプト記には、世界とイスラエル人の歴史が含まれています。それらの本の多くの物語は、教会や新約聖書で参照されています。箴言は、日常生活に簡単に適用できる役に立つ知恵が書かれた書です。

新約聖書には、福音書、初期教会史、初期の教会指導者が書いた手紙、および預言的な書が含まれています。著者のあとに名付けられているマタイ、マルコ、ルカ、ヨハネの福音書はすべてイエスの物語です。これらは新約聖書を読み始めるのに適した書です。使徒の働きは初期の教会の歴史について書かれており、ローマ人への手紙からユダの手紙はすべて教会に対し教え、啓発するために書かれた手紙です。ヨハネの黙示録は、終わりの時に関する預言書です。

THE BOOKS OF THE BIBLE
聖書の書

THE OLD TESTAMENT (旧約聖書)			
1. Genesis	創世記	21. Ecclesiastes	伝道者の書
2. Exodus	出エジプト記	22. Song of Solomon	雅歌
3. Leviticus	レビ記	23. Isaiah	イザヤ書
4. Numbers	民数記	24. Jeremiah	エレミヤ書
5. Deuteronomy	申命記	25. Lamentations	哀歌
6. Joshua	ヨシュア記	26. Ezekiel	エゼキエル書
7. Judges	士師記	27. Daniel	ダニエル書
8. Ruth	ルツ記	28. Hosea	ホセア書
9. 1 Samuel	サムエル記第一	29. Joel	ヨエル書
10. 2 Samuel	サムエル記第二	30. Amos	アモス書
11. 1 Kings	列王記第一	31. Obadiah	オバデヤ書
12. 2 Kings	列王記第二	32. Jonah	ヨナ書
13. 1 Chronicles	歴代誌第一	33. Micah	ミカ書
14. 2 Chronicles	歴代誌第二	34. Nahum	ナホム書
15. Ezra	エズラ記	35. Habakkuk	ハバクク書
16. Nehemiah	ネヘミヤ 記	36. Zephaniah	ゼパニヤ書
17. Esther	エステル 記	37. Haggai	ハガイ書
18. Job	ヨブ 記	38. Zechariah	ゼカリヤ書
19. Psalms	詩篇	39. Malachi	マラキ書
20. Proverbs	箴言		

THE NEW TESTAMENT (新約聖書)			
40. Matthew	マタイの福音書	54. 1 Timothy	テモテへの手紙第一
41. Mark	マルコの福音書	55. 2 Timothy	テモテへの手紙第二
42. Luke	ルカの福音書	56. Titus	テトスへの手紙
43. John	ヨハネの福音書	57. Philemon	ピレモンへの手紙
44. Acts	使徒の働き	58. Hebrews	ヘブル人への手紙
45. Romans	ローマ人への手紙	59. James	ヤコブの手紙
46. 1 Corinthians	コリント人への手紙第一	60. 1 Peter	ペテロの手紙第一
47. 2 Corinthians	コリント人への手紙第二	61. 2 Peter	ペテロの手紙第二
48. Galatians	ガラテヤ人への手紙	62. 1 John	ヨハネの手紙第一
49. Ephesians	エペソ人への手紙	63. 2 John	ヨハネの手紙第二
50. Philippians	ピリピ人への手紙	64. 3 John	ヨハネの手紙第三
51. Colossians	コロサイ人への手紙	65. Jude	ユダの手紙
52. 1 Thessalonians	テサロニケ人への手紙第一	66. Revelation	ヨハネの黙示録
53. 2 Thessalonians	テサロニケ人への手紙第二		

Christian Vocabulary List
キリスト教語彙録

The purpose of this section is to help the reader to better understand Christian terms. Christians use words and discuss concepts from the Bible that may sound foreign to people who are new to reading it. Please ask question about terms you do not understand.

このセクションの目的は、読者がキリスト教の用語をよりよく理解できるようにすることです。クリスチャンは聖書からの言葉を引用し、聖書を読むのが初めての人には外国語のように聞こえるかもしれない概念を使い、話すことがあります。わからない用語があれば、グループリーダーに質問してください。

INTRODUCTION
はじめに

BIBLE (聖書)
This is the Christian holy book. It was given to people by God. It has no flaws. It contains truth, wisdom, guidance, historical documentation, and the words of Jesus.
聖書はクリスチャンの聖なる本です。それは神によって人々に与えられました。間違ったことは一つもありません。それは真実、知恵、導き、歴史的記録、そしてイエスの言葉を含んでいます。

GOSPEL (福音)
The gospel refers to the "good news" of the story of Jesus and the free gift of salvation.
福音は、イエスの物語である「よい知らせ」と無償の贈り物である救いを指しています。

CRUCIFIED (十字架にかけられる)
Crucifixion was an ancient form of execution in which the criminal was nailed or bound to a cross. Jesus, the innocent Son of God, was nailed to the cross as part of God's divine plan to take the punishment that was due to mankind because of sin.
十字架刑は、犯罪者が十字架に釘で打ち付けられるか、縛られて行われた古代の処刑方法でした。罪のない神の御子イエスは、人々の罪のために罰を受けるという神の計画の一部として十字架に釘付けにされました。

WEEK 1
1 週目

CREATOR (創造主)
This is a name referring to God, because He created the world.
神は世界を造られた方であるため、神を指す名前です。

CREATION (創造物、被造物)
This is a name referring to the world and everything in it, which God created.
創造物（被造物）は、神が創造した世界とその中のすべてを指します。

WEEK 2
2 週目

GOD (神)
There is one true God. He exists as three-in-one: The Father, the Son, and the Holy Spirit.
真の神は唯一です。神は、父、子、聖霊の 3 つの位が一体として構成されています。

LORD (主)
Lord is a title of respect for a master or person of authority. This is a term used to address Jesus or to refer to God.
主とは、主人または権威者を尊重する称号です。これは、イエスを指したり、神に言及するために使用される用語です。

WEEK 3
3 週目

DEATH (死)
Death can refer to physical death, that all people face, or the spiritual death that awaits those who do not repent. Those who believe in Jesus will be saved and spend eternity in heaven with God. Those who reject Jesus will be cast into the lake of fire to face a second death. This punishment will last forever.
死とは、すべての人が直面する肉体的な死、または悔い改めない人を待つ霊的な死を指します。イエスを信じる者は救われ、天国で永遠に神と共に過ごします。イエスを拒否する人々は、火の池に追放され、二度目の死と直面します。この罰は永遠に続きます。

SIN (罪)

Sin is wrongdoing against God or others. The Bible reveals what God considers to be sin. Sins are not just severe crimes. For example, telling a lie, being impatient, and being unkind to others are also sins.

罪とは、神や他の人に対して過ちを行うことです。聖書は、神が何を罪とみなすかを明らかにしています。罪は、重大な犯罪のことばかりではありません。例えば、嘘をついたり、苛立ったり、他人に不親切であったりすることも罪です。

ORIGINAL SIN (原罪)

"Original sin" refers to the specific sin of Adam and Eve in the Garden of Eden, which was the first sin that humans committed. They disobeyed God. They ate fruit from a tree that God had forbidden them to eat. All of mankind inherited the consequences of this sin, and since that time every person has committed more sins.

「原罪」とは、エデンの園でのアダムとエバの特定の罪を指します。彼らの犯した罪は人類史上初めての罪でした。彼らは神に従いませんでした。彼らは、神が食べることを禁じた木の実を食べました。人類全員がこの罪の結果を受け継ぎ、その時以来、すべての人がさらなる罪を犯し続けています。

WEEK 4
4 週目

JESUS (イエス)

Jesus is the Son of God and He is God (John 1:18). While He was on earth, Jesus was fully man and fully God. He is perfect and has never sinned. He came down from heaven to save mankind from eternal condemnation. He gave His life as a sacrifice for our sins when He died on the cross. All who believe in Him are saved.

イエスは神の息子であり、また神です（ヨハネの福音書 1 章 18 節）。地上にいた間、イエスは完全に人間であり、完全に神でした。完璧であり、決して罪を犯しませんでした。彼は人類を永遠の罰から救うために天から降りてきました。イエスは十字架で死を迎えたとき、私たちの罪の犠牲としてご自分の命を捧げました。イエスを信じるすべての人は救われます。

SALVATION (救い)

Salvation refers to the freedom that Jesus offers from condemnation. Jesus saved us from death by giving His life for us. Salvation is freely given, but it must be received through faith.

救いとは、イエスが与えてくださる罰からの解放を指します。イエスは私たちのためにご自身のいのちを捧げることによって私たちを死から救ってくださいました。救いは惜しみなく与えられますが、信仰を通して受けとらなければなりません。

RESURRECTION (復活)

Resurrection is coming back from the dead. God has the power to bring people back from the dead, even today. Jesus rose from the dead after three days in His tomb. He also brought people back from the dead when He was on earth.

復活とは死からよみがえることです。神は、今日でも、人々を死からよみがえらせる力を持っています。墓にいたイエスは三日後に死からよみがえりました。彼はまた地上にいたときに、人々を死からよみがえらせました。

REPENT (悔い改める)

Repenting is acknowledging that you have sinned and are in need of forgiveness. It also means turning away from sin instead of continuing to do it. A repentant person is not simply sorry, but actively seeks to leave sin behind. We are to repent for our sins against God and ask Him for His forgiveness. When we humble ourselves before God, He forgives us (1 John 1:9).

悔い改めとは、あなたが罪を犯し、そして赦しを必要としていることを認めることです。また、罪を犯し続けるのではなく、罪から離れることを意味します。悔い改めた人は、単に後悔するだけでなく、積極的に罪から離れようとします。私たちは神に対する罪を悔い改め、神の赦しを求めるべきです。神の前で謙虚になると、神は私たちを赦してくださいます（ヨハネの手紙第一1章9節）。

WEEK 5
5週目

ETERNAL LIFE (永遠の命)

Eternal life refers to the life after death, that lasts forever, which we can experience in heaven. If we believe in Jesus and receive salvation, we can spend an eternity with God, dwelling in His glorious presence.

永遠の命とは、私たちが天国で経験することができる、永遠に続く、死後の人生を指します。私たちがイエスを信じて救いを受けるならば、私たちは神の輝かしい存在の中に住みながら、神と共に永遠に過ごすことができます。

JUDGMENT (裁き)

All people will face judgment for every thought, word, and deed from their lifetime. Each person is responsible for his or her own life and will stand before Jesus to be held accountable.

すべての人は生涯の中でのあらゆる考え、言葉、行為に対して裁きに直面します。各人は自分の人生に責任を持ち、イエスの前に立ち、その責任を問われます。

HEAVEN (天国)

Heaven is a beautiful place where we can be with God forever. There is no more death, mourning or pain (Revelation 21:4).

天国は私たちが永遠に神と共にあることができる美しい場所です。もはや死はなく、悲しみも、叫び声も、苦しみもありません。（ヨハネの黙示録 21 章 4 節）。

HELL (地獄)

"Hell," also referred to as the "lake of fire," is the place of eternal death and separation from God. Those who reject God will be cast into the lake of fire.

「地獄」とも呼ばれる「火の池」は、永遠の死と、神からの分離を意味する場所です。神を拒む者は火の池に投げ込まれます。

WEEK 6
6 週目

FAITH (信仰)

Having faith is believing and trusting in God. It is a choice and a condition of the heart. Having faith in God means believing what He says, trusting that He is good, and knowing that He cares.

信仰を持つことは、神を信じて信頼することを意味します。それは選択と心の状態です。神を信じるということは、神の言うことを信じること、神が善であることを信じること、そして自分を気にかけて下さっていることを知ることを意味します。

BELIEVE (信じること)

This is another word for having faith. Belief can be declared with words, experienced in the heart, and expressed through actions. Choices and actions are a reflection of one's beliefs.

これは信仰を持つということの別の言い方です。信念とは、言葉で宣言したりして、心の中で経験し、行動を通して表現することができます。選択と行動はその人の信念を反映します。

WEEK 7
7 週目

GRACE (恵み)

Grace is unmerited favor. God shows people grace by freely giving love, salvation, and forgiveness, which are not earned or deserved.

恵みとは私たちには受けるに相応しくない恩恵です。神は、受け取る価値や資格の無い私たちに、惜しみない愛、救い、赦しを与えることで、恵みを示されています。

THE LAW (律法)

The Law in the Bible refers to the commands that God gave to His people. He gave Moses commandments for the Israelites to follow.

聖書の律法とは、神が神の民に与えられた命令のことを指しています。神はイスラエル人達が従うための戒律をモーセに与えました。

WORKS (働き)

Some people try to do good things to earn favor. They believe that if they do enough good works, they will go to heaven. However, salvation is offered through grace alone by faith, and not by works.

好意を勝ち取るために良いことをしようとする人もいます。彼らは、十分良いことを行えば天国に行くと信じています。しかしながら救いは、行いによってではなく、信仰により、恵みによってのみ与えられます。

WEEK 8
8週目

SCRIPTURE (聖句)

Scripture refers to the written word of God, which is compiled in the Bible. All Scripture is from God and useful for teaching, rebuking, correcting and training in righteousness.

聖句とは、聖書にまとめられている、神の言葉が書かれたものを指しています。すべての聖句は神の息が吹き込まれたものであり、正しいことを教え、戒め、修正し、義を訓練するのに役立ちます。

PRAYER (祈り)

Prayer is communication with God. It can happen anywhere, anytime, and is not restricted to certain words or types of prayer. This is different than prayer in other religions, which is often only done at a specific location or in a specific way.

祈りとは神とのコミュニケーションです。いつでもどこでも行うことができ、特定の言葉や祈りの種類に限定されません。これは、多くの場合、特定の場所または特定の方法でのみ祈ることができる他の宗教の祈りとは異なります。

MEDITATION (瞑想、黙想)

Meditation in Christianity means thinking deeply. Meditating on Scripture is thinking about the meaning and significance of what the verse or passage says.

キリスト教の瞑想（黙想）とは、深く考えることを意味します。聖句を黙想することは、聖句の意味や意義について考えることです。

Teacher's Guide
リーダーのためのガイド

PREPARE THE GROUP (グループを準備する)

Thank you for your willingness to teach! Before you start this study, there are a few things you should do to help prepare your group:

1. OBTAIN BIBLES: Make sure each person has a Bible. Help them to get a paper copy in their native language. Ensure it is a good translation. Some translations are difficult to understand or may not translate the material as accurately. Also, teach them how to access it digitally on their phones, through a website or through the Bible App.

2. INTRODUCE THE BIBLE: Explain a little bit about the Bible and the different books in it, so they know what they are looking at. Teach them how to look up books, chapters, passages and verses.

3. ESTABLISH THE LEARNING ENVIRONMENT: Encourage group members to ask questions. Let them know that you are here to serve and help them. They may feel insecure about their lack of knowledge.

喜んで教えようという心に感謝します！この学びを開始する前に、グループの準備をサポートするために行うべきことがいくつかあります。

1. 聖書を入手する：各々が聖書を持っていることを確認してください。彼らが母国語の聖書を手にできるよう手伝ってください。その聖書が良い翻訳であることを確認してください。一部の翻訳は理解し難いか、資料を正確に翻訳できていない場合があります。また、ウェブサイトまたは聖書アプリを介して、スマートフォンでデジタル版の聖書にアクセスする方法を教えてください。

2. 聖書の紹介：聖書とその中の様々な本について少し説明して、彼らが何を見ているのかを分かるように指導してください。書、章、節を調べる方法を教えてください。

3. 学ぶ環境を整える：メンバーの方たちに質問するよう勧め、促してください。メンバーのために奉仕し、手伝うためにあなたがいるということを伝えてください。彼らは自分の知識不足について不安を感じているかもしれません。

LEAD THE GROUP
グループを導く

As you go through the study, be flexible and adjust to the needs of your group. Follow the Lord's leading. Make sure group members feel comfortable asking questions and fully understand the content. Here is a format you can use to lead your class:

1. INTRODUCTIONS: Go around the group and have new members introduce themselves to one another.

2. PRAYER REQUESTS: Ask the group members to share praises, prayer requests and additional prayer requests specifically focused on developing their relationship with God (ex- Help believing, obeying, or for God to reveal more of Himself to them).

3. OPENING PRAYER: Open up with prayer. Ask God to lead your time together. After a few sessions, give your group members a chance to pray. One person could give a general prayer for the group, or each person could pray for the person to their right. If they are not sure how to pray, teach them.

4. REVIEW THE HOMEWORK: Review the homework and summarize the reading. Answer their questions. Some of the content may require further explanation or examples.

5. FACILITATE THE DISCUSSION: Encourage participation from all group members. Their answers reveal their level of understanding. Stop to ask if they have questions. Make sure they understand the main points of the lesson and know how to apply it to their lives.

6. WEEKLY CHALLENGE: Explain the weekly challenge in the "Live It Out" section to them. This is a way they can live out the lesson. Follow up with them about the weekly challenge from the previous week as well.

7. CLOSING PRAYER: Close out the group discussion time with a prayer. You can ask specific members if they would be willing to close the group in prayer, to help them grow more comfortable with praying.

8. BE AVAILABLE: Stick around after the study for anyone who would like to ask questions or talk more about the lesson.

LEAD THE GROUP
グループを導く

　学習を進める際には、グループのニーズに合わせて調整し、柔軟に対応してください。主の導きに従ってください。質問をしやすいと思えているか、また内容を完全に理解していることを確認してください。クラスをリードする形式を次に示します。

1. はじめに：グループ内で、お互いに新しいメンバーを紹介しあいます。

2. 祈りのリクエスト：グループメンバーに、賛美や感謝、祈りのリクエスト、特に神との関係の発展に焦点を当てた追加の祈りのリクエストを共有してもらいましょう（例：信じること、従うこと、または神様がご自身をもっと明らかにされるように助けてください）。

3. 始まりの祈り：祈りで始めます。共に過ごす時間を神がくださるよう求めてください。数回のセッションの後、グループメンバーに祈りの機会を与えてみましょう。一人が全体に対して祈っても良いですし、一人ひとりが自分の右側の人のために祈っても良いでしょう。祈る方法がわからない場合は教えてあげましょう。

4. 宿題の確認：宿題を復習し、読んだ部分を要約します。質問があった場合は答えてください。内容によっては、さらなる説明または例を必要とする場合があります。

5. ディスカッションの促し：グループメンバー全員が参加できるよう励まします。解答は、個々の理解のレベルを明らかにします。時々質問があるかどうかを確かめるため、ディスカッションを中断してください。学びの要点を理解し、それを自分の生活に適用する方法を知っているかどうか確認してください。

6. 毎週の課題：「活かしましょう」のセクション内の毎週の課題について説明します。これは、一人ひとりが学びを活用することのできる方法です。前週学んだ課題についてもフォローアップします。

7. 終わりの祈り：グループディスカッションの時間を祈りで締めくくります。特定のメンバーに閉会の祈りをしたいかどうかたずね、祈りに成長し易い環境を作りましょう。

8. 会話が続けられるために環境を作る：質問をしたり、もっと話したい人がいる場合に備えて、学びの後も、少し残りましょう。

LEAD BEYOND THE CLASSROOM
クラスルーム外での導き

This workbook is just a tool to assist you in discipling others. It is only a small part of your relationship with them. Go beyond the classroom. Be a helper and a mentor. Jesus did not limit His teaching to a classroom. He treated His disciples like family.

1. PRAY: Keep praying for them throughout the week. Teach them to pray to God and for one another. Ask them to pray for you.

2. FOLLOW UP WITH THEM: Check in throughout the week to see how they are doing. Show concern for them. Send them encouraging words and Scripture, especially in areas they mentioned in prayer requests.

3. ORGANIZE GROUP COMMUNICATION: Start a social media group for group members to use to interact with one another throughout the week. Use it to send out encouragement, prayer requests, verses, and updates.

4. SPEND TIME WITH THEM: Plan a potluck at your house or at a park. Go hiking together. Consider their interests and hobbies. If one of the group members teaches an art class, plan a time with the group to visit them.

5. BE A FRIEND: Your group members are not just students. They are new friends. Be available for them. Welcome them into your life. Have them over for dinner or go out for coffee. Express an interest in their lives and get to know their families.

6. HELP AND ENCOURAGE THEM: Be there for your group members during their hard times. Pray for them, encourage them, and help them learn how to seek answers and guidance from the Lord.

7. BE AN EXAMPLE: Your students will learn a lot by watching your example. Don't just tell them about the Bible. Show it to them by the way you live. If you treat others with love and grace, they will understand the concepts better.

LEAD BEYOND THE CLASSROOM
クラスルーム外での導き

　　このワークブックは、他の人を弟子訓練するのに役立てるためのツールにすぎません。この学びはあなたとグループとの関係のほんの一部です。教室内の関係にとどまらずにそれ以上に関係を築き上げてください。ヘルパーやメンターになりましょう。イエスは教えを教室に限定せず、弟子を家族のように扱いました。

1. 祈り：一週間を通してメンバーのために祈り続けましょう。神に、そしてお互いのために祈るように教えます。メンバーにあなたのために祈るよう頼みましょう。

2. フォローアップ：週を通してメンバーがどう過ごしているか確認しましょう。グループを気にかけていることを示しましょう。祈りのリクエストがあった場合は特に、励ましの言葉と聖句を送ってください。

3. グループコミュニケーションの立ち上げる：SNS でグループを立ち上げ、次回の集まりまでお互いにコミュニケーションがとれるようにしましょう。グループに励まし、祈りのリクエスト、聖句やアップデートを送り活用しましょう。

4. メンバーと時間を過ごす：あなたの家や公園でグループのためにポットラック（持ち寄りパーティー）を計画してみましょう。一緒にハイキングに行ってもいいでしょう。一人ひとりの興味や趣味を考慮して計画してください。例えば、グループメンバーの 1 人がアートクラスを教えているのなら、グループと一緒に訪問したり参加したりする時間を計画してみましょう。

5. 友達になる：あなたのグループのメンバーは単なる生徒ではなく、新しい友達です。メンバーのために時間を空けてください。あなたの人生に歓迎し招き入れましょう。夕食に誘ったり、コーヒーを飲みに行きましょう。メンバーの人生や生活に興味を示し、また彼らの家族と知り合いましょう。

6. 助け、励ます：グループメンバーが困難な時期にいるとき、一緒にいてください。その人のために祈り、励まし、祈り、聖書、主からの答えと導きを探し求める方法を学べるよう手伝ってください。

7. 模範となる：あなたの生き様から生徒はたくさん学ぶことができます。単に聖書のことだけ伝えるのではなく、自分の生き方から聖書の教えを見せましょう。あなたが他の人を愛と恵みを持って接していれば、教えの意味がより理解しやすくなるでしょう。

CROSS-CULTURAL DISCIPLESHIP
クロスカルチャー訓練

The cultural background of your students influences their understanding of the Bible. Make sure they understand the meaning of the words you are using. Concepts that seem simple may require further explanation for them. Encourage them to ask questions and be prepared to go back to the basics.

Your students will grow tremendously just by spending time reading and studying the Bible. Many of the concepts that may be foreign to them will start to make sense as they read through the examples and stories from Scripture.

あなたの生徒が持つ文化的背景は、聖書の理解に影響します。あなたが使っている用語が理解できているか、よく確認してください。簡単に見える概念も、彼らにとってはさらなる説明が必要なことかもしれません。生徒の皆さんに質問をするように促し、また基本に立ち返る心構えをしておきましょう。

生徒は聖書を読み、学ぶだけでも、すばらしく成長します。聖書からの例えや物語を読み進めるにしたがって、最初は異質なものと感じられていた概念も理解ができるものとなり始めます。

AFTER THIS STUDY
この学びの後

After this study, continue investing in the members of your group. Think about where they are in their journey with the Lord and help them to get connected. Recommend a good church and help them stay connected with the Bible study group. Continue spending time with them and praying for and with them. Pray about the next step for the group.

この学びの後も、グループのメンバーに力を注ぎ続けましょう。メンバーが主との歩みのどこにいるかを考え、主とつながりを持てるよう助けましょう。良い教会を勧め、バイブルスタディグループとのつながりを保てるように助けてください。一緒に時間を過ごし、一人ひとりのために祈り続けましょう。グループの次のステップについて祈りましょう。